D1283038

THE RISE OF THE ISRAELITE MONARCHY:
THE GROWTH AND DEVELOPMENT OF I SAMUEL 7-15

SOCIETY OF BIBLICAL LITERATURE
DISSERTATION SERIES

Edited by
Howard C. Kee
and
Douglas A. Knight

Number 27
THE RISE OF THE ISRAELITE MONARCHY:
THE GROWTH AND DEVELOPMENT OF
I SAMUEL 7-15

by
Bruce C. Birch

SCHOLARS PRESS
Missoula, Montana

THE RISE OF THE ISRAELITE MONARCHY:
THE GROWTH AND DEVELOPMENT OF I SAMUEL 7-15

by
Bruce C. Birch

Published by
SCHOLARS PRESS
for
The Society of Biblical Literature

LIBRARY
McCORMICK THEOLOGICAL SEMINARY
1100 EAST 55th STREET
CHICAGO, ILLINOIS 60610

Distributed by

SCHOLARS PRESS
University of Montana
Missoula, Montana 59801

THE RISE OF THE ISRAELITE MONARCHY: THE GROWTH AND DEVELOPMENT OF I SAMUEL 7-15

by

Bruce C. Birch

Wesley Theological Seminary, Washington, D. C.

Ph.D., 1970   Advisor: Brevard S. Childs
Yale University   Readers: Marvin Pope
                                        W. Sibley Towner
                                        S. Dean McBride

Copyright © 1976

by

The Society of Biblical Literature

Library of Congress Cataloging in Publication Data
Birch, Bruce C
  The rise of the Israelite monarchy.

  (Dissertation series ; no. 27)
  Bibliography: p.
  1. Bible. O. T. 1 Samuel VII-XV—Criticism,
interpretation, etc. 2. Kings and rulers—Biblical teaching. I. Title. II. Series:
Society of Bib-
lical Literature. Dissertation series ; no. 27.
BS1325.2.B57   222'.43'07   76-20680
ISBN 0-89130-112-7

Printed in the United States of America
Edwards Brothers, Inc.
Ann Arbor, Michigan 48104

3S
1325.2
.B57

For Judy and Jeremy

And in memory of Christine

TABLE OF CONTENTS

Page

KEY TO ABBREVIATIONS ix

PREFACE xi

CHAPTER I

    INTRODUCTION 1

CHAPTER II

    SAMUEL, SAUL AND THE RISE OF THE ISRAELITE
    MONARCHY, I SAMUEL 7-15 11

    I Samuel 7 11

    I Samuel 8 21

    I Samuel 9:1-10:16 29

    I Samuel 10:17-27 42

    I Samuel 11 54

    I Samuel 12 63

    I Samuel 13 74

    I Samuel 14 85

    I Samuel 15 94

CHAPTER III

    THE GROWTH AND DEVELOPMENT OF I SAMUEL 7-15 131

BIBLIOGRAPHY 159

ABBREVIATIONS

AJSL	American Journal of Semitic Languages
BA	Biblical Archaeologist
BASOR	Bulletin of the American Schools of Oriental Research
BJRL	Bulletin of the John Rylands Library
BR	Biblical Research
BZ	Biblische Zeitschrift
BZAW	Beihefte zur Zeitschrift für die alttestamentliche Wissenschaft
CBQ	Catholic Biblical Quarterly
GK	Gesenius' Hebrew Grammar, edited by E. Kautzsch
HUCA	Hebrew Union College Annual
IB	Interpreter's Bible
ICC	International Critical Commentary
IDB	Interpreter's Dictionary of the Bible
JAOS	Journal of the American Oriental Society
JBL	Journal of Biblical Literature
JJS	Journal of Jewish Studies
JNES	Journal of Near Eastern Studies
JQR	Jewish Quarterly Review
JSS	Journal of Semitic Studies
JTS	Journal of Theological Studies
MT	Masoretic Text
OLZ	Orientalische Literaturzeitung
PEQ	Palestine Exploration Quarterly
RGG[2]	Die Religion in Geschichte und Gegenwart, second edition
StTh	Studia Theologica
TB	Theologische Blätter

TLZ	Theologische Literaturzeitung
TS	Theological Studies
TZ	Theologische Zeitschrift
VT	Vetus Testamentum
ZAW	Zeitschrift für die alttestamentliche Wissenschaft
ZThK	Zeitschrift für Theologie und Kirche

PREFACE

Scholars have long recognized that the Book of I Samuel is crucial for our understanding of the development of the Israelite kingship. It is virtually our only written source for the transition period from tribal league to monarchy. Unfortunately the nature of I Samuel itself makes such an understanding extremely difficult. The complexity of the critical problems of I Samuel is well known and has fostered numerous works aimed at the clarification of these problems. It is obvious to anyone who has read I Samuel that its great variety of materials cannot stem from a single hand. The process through which the book came into its present shape must have been a complex one. This is especially true of those chapters dealing directly with the establishment of Saul as the first king of Israel (7-15). It is here that the greatest historical and theological interest has focused, and it is here that scholars have most often searched for the key to the composition of the book. Since it is our contention that previous theories on the growth and development of this material prove themselves to be inadequate, chapters 7-15 of I Samuel also form the subject of this investigation.

I must express special thanks to Kermit Schoonover who first interested me in the Books of Samuel and to Brevard Childs who directed my work on this material and taught me much in the process. I am grateful to Mickey McGinnis for his help in preparing this volume for the press. Finally, I can only count myself as especially fortunate to have a wife like Judy who has supported me in so many ways through all stages of this project.

B.C.B.

Washington, D.C.
November 13, 1975

CHAPTER I

INTRODUCTION

Any careful examination of the doublets, tensions and
varying points of view in I Samuel will lead to the conclusion
that it is not a literary unity. Thus, it is not surprising
that the early literary critics regarded the book with a great
deal of interest, and their work still provides the foundation
for most modern studies of the book.

As early as Eichhorn[1] and Thenius[2] the hypothesis was advanced that the doublets and tensions of I Samuel could best be
explained by arguing for the existence of whole parallel
strands of material. It remained, however, for the work of
Julius Wellhausen to develop this hypothesis in all its subtle-
ties.[3] In a manner similar to his work on the Pentateuch,
Wellhausen attempted to separate two main sources in I Samuel.[4]
According to Wellhausen, I Samuel 7-15 may be divided into an
"early" and a "late" source. The nucleus of the early source
is to be found in 9:1-10:16 which was joined with the independent traditions in 11:1-11, 15; 13-14 at an early date. This
formed a literary strand characterized by its view of Samuel as
a local seer who rose to fame because he was instrumental in
Saul's rise to the kingship. In 7:1-8:22; 10:17-27; 12:1-25;
15:1-34 Wellhausen found a much later strand of material added
secondarily to the early material by means of passages such as
11:13-14. This "late" source is characterized by its view of
Israel as a theocracy with Samuel as her representative before
God and by its view of the kingship as the sinful request of the
people which Yahweh finally granted. For Wellhausen these
ideas can only have come from the community of post-exilic Ju-
daism; hence, the materials of the "late" source cannot be regarded as having much value for the purposes of historical reconstruction. Wellhausen also argued that because of parallels
to D, the "late" source should be regarded as Deuteronomically
influenced. This secondary strand of material was essentially
an addition to the "early" source to form the narrative which
now appears in I Samuel.

1

The work of Karl Budde represented a new advance in the discussion.[5] He argued strongly for the independence of the two sources from one another, and he further identified the two with the Pentateuchal sources J and E. These two independent sources were combined by a Deuteronomic redactor who also eliminated certain objectionable passages. These passages were, however, brought back into the book by a later hand in a slightly altered arrangement. Although many accepted Budde's argument for the independence of the early and late sources, his identification of these with J and E received only limited support. There did result from Budde's work a tendency to assign an earlier date to the late source, an argument Budde was forced to make because of his identification of the late source with E.

The general consensus of scholarship at the turn of the century is perhaps best represented by the commentary of H. P. Smith in 1902.[6] The emphasis rests heavily on documentary analysis, and the entire book of I Samuel is confidently divided between the early and late sources. These two sources are accepted, following Budde, as independent documents, but are not identified with J and E. The Deuteronomic writer found these sources already combined and found its viewpoint congenial enough that only minor editorial changes and additions were necessary. Smith accepted, along with most others at this time, Wellhausen's contention that the early source was to be regarded as much more trustworthy for historical purposes than the late source.

The work of Hugo Gressmann stands in distinct contrast to the majority of scholars at the turn of the century.[7] He advanced a hypothesis for the composition of I Samuel that might best be characterized as a fragmentary view. He argued that the book was loosely put together by a late editorial hand from a great variety of independent narrative units of varying sizes. He denied that these had in any way come together in what might be called sources or strands, and then concentrated on the analysis of individual narratives. Few have accepted his analysis since he leaves the manner in which these narratives came together without adequate explanation. However, his contributions to the study of the individual narratives have been very influential.

The widespread consensus at the turn of the century has not held up under the impact of more recent studies on I Samuel. Although a few have defended an analysis along the lines of Wellhausen,[8] most have felt that a two-source theory is not adequate to explain the origin of this material. As a result, many scholars have advanced multiple source theories for the composition of I Samuel. A. Lods has argued that the early source is itself a composite of two independent sources: a 'seer' source beginning with the tale of Saul's search for the lost asses and a Jabesh source which originally began with a story of Saul's birth which has been transferred to Samuel.[9] R. H. Pfeiffer subdivided the late source because he felt the literary unevenness he detected there indicated multiple authorship.[10] A. R. S. Kennedy divides both the early and the late source and finds four different strands in I Samuel.[11] More recently, Weiser has divided the sources into complexes of tradition based on their connections to different geographical locales.[12] A similar approach has been adopted by Hertzberg and Schunck.[13] The identification of the early and late sources with J and E now receives very little support[14] although Eissfeldt, in particular, remains a vigorous defender of this hypothesis, finding in I Samuel not only J and E but also his earlier L source.[15] None of the various subdivisions of the material have been able to achieve widespread support.

Since the identification of the early and late sources with J and E received no widespread support, most scholars have returned to a later date for the late source, and this has resulted in renewed attention to its relationship with the work of the Deuteronomist. At the very least scholars are inclined to view the materials attributed to the late source as stemming from circles possessing interests similar to those of the Deuteronomist (Smith, Pfeiffer, Caird). This is especially true in the matter of what is judged to be an anti-monarchical attitude in the late source materials. Others argue that the material usually attributed to the late source is the actual work of the Deuteronomist who imposed his anti-monarchical theology onto older material more positive to the kingship. The most

influential argument for the latter view was made by Martin
Noth in his study of the Deuteronomistic history work.[16]

Noth argues that the historical books from Joshua through
II Kings have been edited into a single work by a Deuteronomistic historian who has imposed his own theological perspective
onto the material by means of the framework into which he fits
the older traditions. He has then prefaced this work with the
Book of Deuteronomy to which he wrote a new preface (1:1-4:43).
In general it is the policy of this Deuteronomistic historian
not to rewrite extensively the materials he uses. Noth prefers
to speak of various units of tradition rather than sources or
strands. In I Samuel 7-15 he finds materials from an old Saul
tradition in 9:1-10:16 and 10:27b-11:15. At a later time the
independent traditions in chapters 13, 14 and 15 were added.
The remaining materials (7:2-17; 8:1-22; 10:17-27a; 12:1-25)
are labeled by Noth as Deuteronomistic insertions. Further
these passages represent a more active role on the part of the
Deuteronomistic historian than elsewhere (presumably because of
the crucial nature of this period dealing with the rise of
kingship). These passages constitute either the original constructions of the Deuteronomist (8 and 12) or the thorough re-
vision of older traditions from a Deuteronomistic viewpoint (7
and 10:17ff.). It has been observed that Noth's analysis bears
considerable similarity to the work of Wellhausen, although not
without its own original contribution.[17] Noth is, however,
considerably more cautious than Wellhausen on two matters.
First, he is not at all so certain that the older traditions
can be used to reconstruct the authentic history of the period.
He warns that these traditions have been obscured by folkloristic and anecdotal elements. Secondly, Noth does not believe
that one can talk about a single early source, and instead
stresses the multiplicity of early traditions. It was the Deuteronomistic historian that brought the traditions together in
their present form, according to Noth.

Although Noth's hypothesis of a Deuteronomistic history
work is suggestive, his work on I Sam. 7-15 must be the subject
of some objection. Throughout this section the main basis for
assigning sections to the Deuteronomist seems to be the presup-
position that opposition to kingship is late and reflects

Israel's bad experience with her kings, and that Samuel's role there is one that could not have existed in the early tradition. Both might be open to debate, and Noth does little in the way of detailed analysis of language or form to support his case.

It can be said that for the most part recent scholarship on the growth and development of I Samuel is still heavily reliant on some form of the two-source hypothesis (early and late source). A larger number of scholars, influenced by Noth's work, are emphasizing the importance of Deuteronomistic influence in the materials usually attributed to the late source. However, despite this general agreement, the various attempts to trace out these two sources and explain their relationship remain at complete variance and are decidedly unconvincing. Recently a few scholars have suggested that between the old traditions and the work of the Deuteronomist there was a middle stage of editorial activity. The nature of this pre-Deuteronomistic stage has only been vaguely identified as prophetic, and there is yet to be a detailed attempt to analyze the nature of this editorial work. Weiser merely suggests that there was a "prophetic interpretation of the history and its traditions which proceeds side by side with the traditions of the people and the court, though it also stands in antithesis to them."[18] Although these narratives grow out of a similar intellectual and theological context Weiser insists that they do not constitute a literary unity.[19] Fohrer has advanced a similar position.[20] Knierim has supported the existence of a pre-Deuteronomistic editing in prophetic circles and has attempted in an article to discuss its theological perspective.[21] Although this view holds promise for a way out of the impasse on the critical issues of I Sam. 7-15 the detailed analysis of the material to see if such a pre-Deuteronomistic edition can be shown remains yet to be done.

In summary it can be agreed that I Samuel 7-15 shows ample evidence of a complex process of growth and development involving a wide variety of materials, but source analysis has not been successful in unraveling this process. Although some form of a two source theory has been the usual approach, scholars

have reached no consensus on the contents or character of these
sources. For the most part attempts to find the key to the
origins of I Sam. 7-15 have been marred by the presuppositions
of the investigators. Early work in I Samuel was hindered by
the presumption that documentary analysis which seemed so successful in Pentateuchal studies was the key to I Samuel as
well. Notions of the way in which Israelite religion developed
also served to predetermine the results of a critical examination of I Samuel. More recently scholars have tended to allow
conceptions of the supposed, actual course of events to make
judgment on the date of traditions. The idea that certain theological conceptions, such as the dim view of the monarchy,
could only be late developments has substituted for close analysis of the text. Few studies have not been marred by literary, historical or theological presuppositions that predetermine the results to some extent.

Most of the work on I Sam. 7-15 has proceeded on the task
of constructing theories of overall composition without the
benefit of a careful analysis of the individual units of tradition. Our purpose in this study is to start with a close examination of the materials in I Sam. 7-15 and let this determine the direction we move in constructing a larger theory of
composition. Our process of analysis shall proceed as follows:
We shall carefully analyze the various units of tradition within I Sam. 7-15 in order to determine as much as possible concerning the formal structures in which this material is preserved, the circles in which it was preserved and its original
function. Only then can we ask how the various tradition complexes have been ordered and related to one another. If indeed
there are relationships between various materials we must ask
whether these relationships are indicative of various editorial
levels within the process through which I Samuel 7-15 came into
its present shape. We wish to examine each tradition complex
in its own right, but it is also important that the final form
in which we have received the traditions be taken seriously.

We believe that the analysis of the various pericopes in
I Sam. 7-15 will allow us to escape the necessity of presuppos-
ing theories of composition. In fact, it is our belief that

the outline of a logical schema shows itself clearly and solves
many of the problems which marred previous hypotheses. In a
final chapter we will attempt to outline the process of growth
and development which brought these chapters into their present
form. In doing so we hope to illumine the methods, viewpoints
and purposes which characterized the various stages in this
process.

CHAPTER I

[1]J. G. Eichhorn, *Einleitung in das Alte Testament*, 4th edition (Göttingen: 1823-24), III, pp. 464-533.

[2]Otto Thenius, *Kommentar zu den Samuelisbüchern* (1842).

[3]The contributions of J. Wellhausen to the study of I Samuel are found in three works: *Der Text der Bücher Samuelis* (Göttingen: Vandenhoeck und Ruprecht, 1872); *Die Composition des Hexateuchs und der historischen Bücher des Alten Testaments* (Berlin: 1899); and *Prolegomena to the History of Ancient Israel*, translated by Menzies and Black (New York: Meridian, 1957, original German edition 1878).

[4]Wellhausen, *Prolegomena*, pp. 245-272.

[5]Karl Budde, *Die Bücher Richter und Samuel, ihre Quellen und ihre Aufbau* (Tübingen: J. C. B. Mohr, 1890).

[6]H. P. Smith, *A Critical and Exegetical Commentary on the Books of Samuel*, ICC (New York: Charles Scribner's Sons, 1902).

[7]Hugo Gressmann, *Die älteste Geschichtsschreibung und Prophetie Israels von Samuel bis Amos und Hosea*, in *Die Schriften des Alten Testaments*, part 2, vol. 1 (Göttingen: Vandenhoeck und Ruprecht, 1921).

[8]For example, R. de Vaux, *Les Livres de Samuel* (Paris, 1953), pp. 9ff.; and A. Bentzen, *Introduction to the Old Testament*, vol. II, second edition (Copenhagen: G. E. C. Gad, 1952), pp. 91ff.

[9]A. Lods, *Israel from its Beginnings to the Middle of the Eighth Century*, translated by S. H. Hooke (New York: Alfred Knopf, 1948), pp. 352ff. So also W. A. Irwin, "Samuel and the Rise of the Monarchy," *AJSL*, 58 (1941), pp. 113ff.

[10]R. H. Pfeiffer, *Introduction to the Old Testament*, revised edition (New York: Harper and Brothers, 1941), pp. 359ff.

[11]A. R. S. Kennedy, *Samuel. The New Century Bible* (New York: Henry Frowde, 1905), pp. 13ff.

[12]A. Weiser, *Samuel: Seine geschichtliche Aufgabe und religiöse Bedeutung* (Göttingen: Vandenhoeck und Ruprecht, 1962). This approach has, however, been rightly criticized as failing to consider the close proximity of these locations to one another, thus making it difficult to consider locale as the basic distinguishing feature of different tradition complexes. See the review by S. Herrmann in *TLZ*, 89 (1964), pp. 819ff.

[13]H. W. Hertzberg, *I and II Samuel*, translated by J. S. Bowden (Philadelphia: Westminster Press, 1964). Klaus-Dietrich Schunck, *Benjamin*, *BZAW* 86 (Berlin: Alfred Töpelmann, 1963).

[14]See N. Snaith, "The Historical Books," *The Old Testament and Modern Study*, edited by H. H. Rowley (Oxford: Oxford University Press, 1956), pp. 99ff., for a survey of recent opinion on the matter.

[15]O. Eissfeldt, *Die Komposition der Samuelisbücher* (Leipzig: J. C. Hinrichs, 1931); and *The Old Testament: An Introduction*, translated by P. Ackroyd (New York: Harper and Row, 1965), pp. 271ff.

[16]Martin Noth, *Überlieferungsgeschichtliche Studien*, second edition (Tübingen: Max Niemeyer, 1957).

[17]Discussed by Paul A. Riemann, "The Sources for the Establishment of the Kingship in I Samuel," unpublished paper, Graduate Seminar, Harvard University, 1959, p. 8.

[18]A. Weiser, *The Old Testament: Its Formation and Development*, translated by Dorothea M. Barton (New York: Association Press, 1961), p. 166.

[19]*Ibid.*

[20]Sellin-Fohrer, *Einleitung in das Alte Testament*, tenth edition (Heidelberg: Quelle und Meyer, 1965), pp. 242ff.

[21]R. Knierim, "The Messianic Concept in the First Book of Samuel," *Jesus and the Historian*, edited by F. Thomas Trotter (Philadelphia: Westminster Press, 1968).

CHAPTER II

SAMUEL, SAUL AND THE RISE OF THE ISRAELITE MONARCHY - I SAM. 7-15

In studying the development of the materials on the early Israelite monarchy it is difficult to determine what the limits of the study will be. The chapters chosen for this discussion have obvious connections with material both before and after them in the Book of First Samuel. However, chapters 7-15 represent the closest that one can come to a self-contained section on the very establishment of the kingship in Israel. Although Saul is still nominally king in chapters 16ff., it has long been recognized that this is essentially a history of the rise of David. Saul's fate as king is sealed in the account of chapter 15. Similarly the early chapters of I Samuel would be helpful if one were to undertake a study of Samuel, but the kingship itself is not an issue until chapter 8. Chapter 7 is often left out in treatments of Saul and the beginnings of monarchy in Israel. To be sure, it does not explicitly mention either Saul or the institution of kingship, but it will be our contention that in the overall arrangement this chapter plays an important introductory role. In this chapter we shall examine each section of material closely in an attempt to see the patterns of growth and development which brought chapters 7-15 into their present shape.

I Samuel 7

Earlier attempts to find source strands in I Samuel have generally placed chapter 7 in the late source.[1] Some scholars would see the chapter as having been subsequently reshaped or added to by the Deuteronomist.[2] Martin Noth, in his hypothesis of a Deuteronomistic history work, attributes the chapter as a whole to the work of the Deuteronomist although he agrees that vss. 15-17 may reflect knowledge of an old tradition recalling Samuel's "law-speaking" activities.[3] Whether a late source or a Deuteronomistic hand most scholars are agreed that chapter 7 belongs with 8; 10:17-27; 12 as a strand of material emphasizing the role of Samuel, tending to be anti-monarchical and usually unreliable historically. More recently Weiser[4] has argued against Noth that chapter 7 contains old tradition material, but he too limits it to vss. 2-6 and 15-17. The account of the deliverance from the Philistines in vss. 7-14 is a fiction added by a later hand to enhance the image of Samuel. Only a few scholars[5] have considered the battle account in 7:7-14 to have any roots in old and authentic tradition. Despite differences in literary analysis scholars have been generally agreed that in its present form I Sam. 7 functions to portray Samuel as one of the judges, in the sense of deliverer as in the Book of Judges, and to remove the Philistine menace as a possible justification for the establishment of kingship.[6]

The bulk of chapter 7 is set off from the history of the ark by the concluding chronological note in vs. 2.[7] The twenty year figure seems to be a later addition to a note merely indicating an indefinite passage of time. Although it does not fit the chronological formulae used in the Book of Judges (e.g. Jdgs. 3:30b; 5:31b) there is little reason to question the usual interpretation that this figure is a part of the Deuteronomistic chronology as described by Noth.[8]

The chapter is probably not the product of a single hand. Vss. 3 and 5 parallel each other in certain broad respects. Both record an address by Samuel related to a gathering of all Israel, and there is no apparent attempt to explain the second assembly in vs. 5. Vs. 3 opens with a common introduction identifying speaker and party addressed. The speech itself is a conditional command: the protasis is introduced by the particle אִם + a participle with pronominal subject. The apodosis is expressed in a series of three imperatives and concluded with a verbal clause of result. Vs. 4 then uses two waw consecutive + imperfect constructions to record the fulfillment of the conditional command by the Israelites. The appearance in vs. 5 of another identification of Samuel as speaker is unexpected and seems to represent the introduction of a new matter. It should be noted, however, that although v. 4 records the people's fulfillment of the command given by Samuel, the fulfillment of the delivery from the Philistines promised as the result is missing. Although vss. 3-4 seem to be of a somewhat different matter than what follows, their position at this point in the chapter is of significance. It would seem that vss. 3-4 have been placed as an introduction in order that the following tradition of deliverance may function as the fulfillment of the promise. A further evidence that vss. 3-4 were originally independent of vs. 5 may be seen in the fact that the call to repentance in vs. 3 is fulfilled in vs. 4 thus making the ceremony of penance in vs. 5 unnecessary.

The formula וישפט שמואל את-בני ישראל which appears in 6b does not seem to belong to the material preceding or following it. Indeed to say at this point that Samuel 'judged' Israel has little meaning. Certainly nothing in the ceremony of vs. 6 portrays Samuel as a judge. The miraculous victory recorded in vss. 7-12 might suggest the military deliverers called judges in the Book of Judges, but a close reading makes clear that Samuel is not portrayed as a deliverer or warrior in this sense. The same formula appears three times elsewhere in the chapter (vss. 15, 16, and 17). Here it is clear that Samuel is called a judge because of his judicial activities. He travels a circuit administering justice at each station on the route described. It is only in light of this notice that 6bβ can be read. Vs. 6bβ uses the identical formula found in vs. 15 and must be intended as an attempt to link 5-11 to 16-17 since scholars are generally agreed that vss. 16-17 comprise an originally independent tradition unit.

Muilenburg has claimed that all of the Mizpah references in this chapter are secondary additions to the text.[9] It appears only in editorial contexts and is not original to the traditions recorded here. He argues that Mizpah was not a center of worship until after the exile. Against Muilenburg one must say that it is very difficult to ascribe all the references to Mizpah in this chapter to an editorial hand. Its appearance on Samuel's judicial circuit in 7:16 places it side by side with two well-known early cultic centers. There are no literary grounds for challenging the authenticity of the Mizpah reference in this context. On literary grounds the authenticity of the Mizpah references in vss. 11 and 12 are also difficult to challenge. In vs. 12 the use of Mizpah in pinpointing

the exact location of the stone is quite in keeping with the
tendency of aetiological notices to exact topographical design-
nation. The notice in vs. 11 fits smoothly syntactically and
there is little reason to regard Mizpah as an addition here in
light of its appearance in the aetiological notice. The prob-
ability seems great that Mizpah was an important cultic center
in the time of Samuel, and its connection with the tradition of
Samuel's judicial circuit and the tradition of miraculous delivery from the Philistines should be considered as authentic.
Mizpah is probably to be considered original to both traditions, and the hand which added 6bβ simply wished to point out
that Samuel was at Mizpah by reason of his judicial circuit
when the Philistine confrontation occurred, thus the two traditions become linked.

Is the tradition of a ceremony of repentance in vss. 5-6
also originally linked to Mizpah? It is possible, but the actual Mizpah references do not seem too closely allied literarily to the tradition material of the ceremony itself. In vs. 5
Samuel is responsible for the call to assembly קבצו את-כל-ישראל
המצפתה, but strangely he plays no role at all in the rites of
vs. 6. The language of the Mizpah notes in 6aα ויקבצו המצפתה
and 7a כי-התקבצו בני-ישראל המצפתה shows that they are dependent
on the notice of Samuel's summons in 5. Vs. 6a makes the ceremony of repentance a response to Samuel's leadership, and 7a
establishes the identity of two originally separate occasions.
Thus, it is possible that an editorial hand which knew the tradition of Samuel's judicial circuit (16-17), as shown by 6bβ
and 15, has used an assembly at Mizpah called by Samuel to relate two originally independent traditions: one concerning a
ceremony of repentance and the other concerning a miraculous
delivery from the Philistines ending with an aetiological
note.[10] Mizpah was selected as the site of this gathering because the tradition of delivery was already connected with this
site and because Mizpah was known to be one of Samuel's regular
stopping places on his judicial circuit. The evidence for this
is slim, however, and it is also possible that 6a belongs with
7-11 and simply records a ceremony whose nature is now unclear.

As seen previously vss. 3-4 form a separate unit attached
to the beginning of the chapter. Vss. 13-14 have not been

mentioned thus far. It represents a summarizing note clearly distinguishable from the aetiological notice in vs. 12 and the tradition of Samuel's judicial activity in 15-17. Its most striking quality is its extravagant claims for the consequences of the victory in 7-12, but we will reserve discussion of its character for a later point.

Having distinguished the basic units of tradition in I Sam. 7 as much as possible on literary grounds we must now look at the character and setting of these traditions closely before we can draw any further conclusions on the development of this chapter into its present form.

We have had occasion earlier to comment briefly on the formal structure of 7:3-4. The use of the conditional phrase (אִם) should not mislead us here. Although this might suggest to some a relationship to casuistically formulated laws, the affinities of this pericope lie rather with the apodictic formulations. This is seen most clearly in the imperative clauses of the protasis. The conditional clause simply serves to identify the concern toward which these commands are directed--namely return to Yahweh. The result clause which follows indicates the benefit that will result from fulfillment of these commands. A similar conditional construction is seen in Deut. 11:13ff. Here too the conditional identifies the concern of the writer, obedience, and the infinitives which follow express the real conditions which must be met, love and service, in order for the benefits listed in 14ff. to come to pass. Muilenburg is probably right when he lists I Sam. 7:3-4 among the passages he feels reflect covenantal form and structure.[11] The form reflects the stipulations and blessing of the covenant form. However, he also stresses that the influence of covenant forms stretches from early to late times and is capable of great diversity. Thus, the form of I Sam. 7:3-4 cannot of itself help us in identifying the hand responsible for its insertion. We must look at its style and content as well.[12]

The formula הסירו את-אלהי הנכר appears four times in the Old Testament (Gen. 35:2; Jos. 24:23; Jdgs. 10:16; I Sam. 7:3). In all but Jdgs. 10:16 it is an imperative command. Gen. 35: 1-5 certainly represents the oldest tradition setting in which

we find this formula. E. Nielsen has postulated that this reflects an early ritual in which images of the gods of one's
enemies were buried or destroyed.[13] The result is the terror
of God which falls on the enemy in vs. 5. However, except for
the use of the formula itself, I Sam. 7:3-4 really bears little
resemblance to Gen. 35:1-5.[14] Rather its affinities lie with
the passages in Jos. 24:23-24 and Jdgs. 10:6-16.[15] A rough
chart will demonstrate this:

	Gen. 35:1-5		Jos. 24:23-24
(2)	הסרו את-אלהי הנכר	(23)	הסירו את-אלהי הנכר
		(23)	והטו את-לבבכם אל-יהוה
		(24)	את-יהוה אלהינו נעבד

	Jdgs. 10:6-16		I Sam. 7:3-4
(16)	ויסירו את-אלהי הנכר	(3)	הסירו את-אלהי הנכר
		(3)	והכינו לבבכם אל-יהוה
(16)	ועבדו את-יהוה	(3)	ועבדהו לבדו
(6)	את-הבעלים את-העשתרות	(4)	את-הבעלים את-העשתרת

It is clear that the context in which the formula in I Sam. 7:3
stands is closer to that of Jos. 24:23 and Jdgs. 10:16 than to
Gen. 35:2. The formula is now tied to themes expressing the
concern for purity of Yahwistic worship. The foreign gods are
identified as the Baals and Ashtaroth of Canaanite worship, and
their being put aside is to be accompanied by devotion to Yahweh and the rendering of service to him. The original connection of the formula as directed against one's enemies may be
preserved in the close connection of loyalty to Yahweh and holy
war traditions long noted as characteristic of the Deuteronomic
theology.[16] Interestingly Jos. 24:23-24; Jdgs. 10:6-16; and I
Sam. 7:3-4 all stand in close proximity to holy war traditions
either as introductions or conclusions. Furthermore, both Jos.
24:23-24 and Jdgs. 10:6-16 are generally considered to show
Deuteronomistic influence,[17] and it is therefore likely that
I Sam. 7:3-4 is also from a Deuteronomistic hand. The phrase
בכל-לבבכם would seem to support this since it appears only in
relatively late contexts, most of which are Deuteronomistic.[18]

     I Sam. 7:3-4 can probably be considered to be a Deuterono-
mistic introduction to 7:5ff. As such it provides a link

between the disaster described in the ark history (4:1-7:1) and
the victory described later in chapter 7. This link is very
similar in viewpoint to the longer introduction in Jdgs. 10:6-
16 and as we have seen has some formal similarities as well.
The intent of the unit in I Sam. 7:3-4 seems to be to imply
that the disaster when the ark was captured was due to apostasy, and deliverance from the Philistines will now be dependent on a return to Yahweh. The turning back to Yahweh is recorded in vs. 4, and the author evidently intends vss. 5ff. to
be read as the fulfillment of the promised deliverance. Thus,
he has set the following traditions in the same cycle of apostasy, repentance and deliverance well known from the Book of
Judges. This, however, is hardly the original setting for the
tradition material in I Sam. 7:5ff.

The tradition of a cultic ritual of penitence involving
water pouring in vs. 6 is without clear parallel in the Old
Testament. Water is known as a symbol of purity and renewal,
but the pouring of water in connection with a ritual of penitence is not explicitly recorded until Mishnaic records of water pouring in connection with the feast of tabernacles.[19] In
any case the connection with the notice of fasting and the use
of the formula of congregational confession make it clear that
we are dealing with a ritual of penitence. The original setting of this tradition is now obscured. It might well have
been a ceremony originally connected with the sanctuary at Mizpah. As it now stands this verse (6) seems to be representing
this cultic observance as led by Samuel in the course of his
normal duties on his judicial circuit. This simply explains
what Samuel was doing at Mizpah and why the Israelites were
assembled when the Philistines came up against them.[20]

The tradition of miraculous delivery from the Philistines
in I Sam. 7:7-12 seems clearly to be a holy war tradition. The
encounter is prefaced by sacrifice (vs. 9); it is Yahweh himself who fights, calling into service the forces of nature (vs.
10) and throwing the enemy into confusion (vs. 10). These are
among the primary motifs of holy war.[21] The language itself is
the language of holy war. The verb המם appears five times and
always in a holy war context.[22] In all but Jdgs. 4 Yahweh's

victory is accompanied by meteorological phenomena such as
thunder, lightning or hail. W. Richter has suggested that
I Sam. 7:7-12 uses one of two formal types of holy war schema.[23]
This schema is also found in Ex. 14; Jos. 10 and Jdgs. 4.

The prelude:　　　God reassures his people either directly
(Jos. 10:8; Ex. 14:15-18) or through his
prophet (Ex. 14:13-14; Jdgs. 4:14; I Sam.
7:9). In I Sam. 7:9 the actual response
of God is not recorded, but we are told
that he answered in response to Samuel's
entreaty.

The battle:　　　The activity of God himself stands in the
foreground; he confuses the enemy (Ex. 14:
24; Jos. 10:10; Jdgs. 4:15; I Sam. 7:10).

The conclusion: Either לא נשאר עד-אחד (Ex. 14:28; Jdgs.
4:16) or הכה עד (Jos. 10:10; I Sam. 7:11).

Only I Sam. 7:8 records an unbroken call to Yahweh on the part
of the prophet. This would seem to heighten the importance of
the prophetic figure in the tradition, perhaps indicating that
this particular tradition was preserved in circles interested
in the prophetic role of Samuel. Certainly the existence of
prophetic activity in the rites connected with holy war is
known elsewhere (cf. I Kgs. 20:13-14; 22:5-12; II Kgs. 3:11-19).
In this role the prophets can probably be regarded as the suc-
cessors to officials of the tribal league as represented here
by Samuel. The aetiology in 7:12 is probably a record of the
memorial near Mizpah which has served as the focal point for
preservation of this tradition.[24] Thus, we have in 7:7-12 the
tradition of a military encounter with the Philistines couched
in the language of holy war. It was probably originally connected with the cult center of Mizpah and in its present form
seems to emphasize the role of Samuel as the performer of holy
war rites prior to the victory of Yahweh itself. R. Bach has
shown in a recent study[25] that at the time of the establishment
of the Israelite state or shortly thereafter the traditions of
the holy war characteristic of the tribal league were taken up
into prophecy. R. Rendtorff[26] comments along similar lines
that "substantial charismatic functions of the amphictyonic
military leader were clearly taken over, shortly after that
office ceased to exist, by the prophets." The role of Samuel

in this holy war tradition is not that of charismatic deliverer
but of prophetic agent of God's victory in the holy war. Such
an emphasis in the final shape of this old tradition may be due
to preservation in early prophetic circles or at least would
fit in well with their interest in Samuel as an early prophetic
figure.[27]

There would seem to be little to support the claim that
this account of a miraculous victory was created by a late
Deuteronomistic hand. None of the characteristic elements of
the Deuteronomistic style appear here, and there is nothing
that requires us to view this tradition as late. It is not
unlikely that among the skirmishes which must have taken place
between the Philistines and Israelites a minor victory for Israel could have been won which gave rise to this tradition.
The necessity to see this chapter as late and unhistorical
rises in the extravagant claims of vs. 13 and not in the tradition recorded in vss. 7-12. That vss. 13-14 did not originally
connect with vs. 12 may be seen in the conflict between the
limited victory recorded in vss. 11-12 and the claim to have
permanently removed the Philistines from the land in vs. 13.
B. Long, in his study of aetiological forms, also points out
in a brief discussion of I Sam. 7:12[28] that the aetiology in
this verse is clearly a bit of tradition originally independent
of the Deuteronomistic formula for concluding a victory in vs.
13 ('And Yahweh subdued כנע so and so on that day...'). Since
this type of aetiological notice usually forms the concluding
element in an account it must be concluded that it was added
prior to the appending of vss. 13-14.

The concluding summary found in vss. 13-14 has always been
suspect because of the far-reaching effects that are there attributed to the victory over the Philistines. We are told that
they do not again enter ולא יספו עוד לבוא Israel's borders and
that the hand of Yahweh was against them for all of Samuel's
life. Unfortunately these verses have led many to consider the
entire tradition as late and secondary, but as we have seen
vss. 7-12 show no relationship to the excessive claims of 13-
14. In form and vocabulary vs. 13 is similar to the notes
which conclude the deliverance accounts in the Book of Judges.

The verb כנע appears in the niphal only four times elsewhere,[29] and three are in the Deuteronomistic framework to Judges where this subjection formula appears in close connection to the Deuteronomistic chronology. The construction ותהי יד-יהוה ב... is also found mainly in Deuteronomistic contexts.[30] The use of the term Amorite in vs. 14 probably also shows the Deuteronomistic hand. Amorite is the term used by Deuteronomy (and the Elohist) for the pre-Israelite population of the land.[31] The complete subjugation of the Philistines recorded in vs. 14 cannot, of course, be regarded as historical in its present context since we know this was not accomplished until the time of David. This concluding notice in vss. 13-14 has probably been inserted by the same Deuteronomistic hand responsible for vss. 3-4. His intent seems to be to fit the tradition of I Sam. 5-12 into the same framework found in the Book of Judges. To do this he had to insert his concluding notice between vss. 12 and 15 which as we have seen above were probably already connected. Such a position at the end of the battle tradition itself is, however, entirely logical.

Virtually all commentators are agreed that vss. 15-17 preserve an old tradition of Samuel's judicial activities. We have seen earlier, however, that the actual formula of judgeship which appears four times in the chapter (see p. 13) plays a role in the uniting of originally independent traditions. Its appearance in vss. 16-17 may also reflect the hand of this editor but need not call into question the antiquity of the tradition of Samuel's judicial circuit. This editorial hand is not to be identified with the Deuteronomistic hand who added vss. 3-4 and 13-14.

* * *

Our findings might be summarized in a preliminary manner as follows:

A.   Two old traditions which were originally preserved independently of one another are to be found in vss. 5-6abα, 7-12 and 16-17.

B.   A later editorial hand which has joined these traditions can be detected in vss. 6bβ and 15. Samuel the judge is identified with the Samuel who plays a role in the institution

of holy war. It is interesting to note that Deborah also per-
forms judicial functions and yet is closely connected with a
holy war tradition, although as with Samuel she is not the deliverer. We might also note that Deborah is called a prophet-
ess, while Samuel too appears elsewhere in a prophetic role.
Both Rendtorff and Noth[32] have noted that the traditions concerning the charismatic functions of the early prophets do not
rule out a connection and interest in judicial functions as
well. This may give a clue to the identity of those circles
who might have joined the two diverse traditions of I Sam. 7;
however, no solid conclusions can be made on the basis of the
slender evidence which this chapter affords.

C. A Deuteronomistic hand has added an introductory notice in vss. 3-4 and a concluding notice in vss. 13-14. The
form and function seem analogous to the framework of the Book
of Judges. The intent seems to be to depict the victory over
the Philistines as one of the deliverances which follow repentance from apostasy characteristic of the Deuteronomistic view
of the period of the tribal league. There has been no attempt,
contrary to many scholars, to depict Samuel here as the last of
the judge/deliverers. The Deuteronomistic hand has here been
content with additions and seems to have done no reworking of
the materials he found before him.

A brief comment is in order concerning the placement of
this chapter in relation to the material which follows in I
Sam. 8-12. It would seem clear that its placement here is
meant to take some of the force out of the claim that the Philistine crisis required the establishment of a monarchy. However, it is impossible at this point to determine at which
stage in the process described above the chapter was placed
here. A conclusion on the arrangement of material in I Sam.
7-12 must wait until we have examined more of this material in
detail.

I Samuel 8

Since Wellhausen, advocates of both two-source and three-
source theories of composition have agreed that I Sam. 8 belongs to the late source and is, in fact, one of its crucial

chapters.[33] Some of these scholars, including Wellhausen himself, noticed evidence in the chapter of Deuteronomic influence but usually attributed this to secondary editing after the formation of the late source. Martin Noth popularized the notion that the chapter in its entirety should be attributed to the Deuteronomistic hand responsible for the formation of a single historical work stretching from Jos. to Kings.[34] However, both Noth and earlier scholars are agreed that I Sam. 8 is distinctly anti-monarchical in tone and arose late in Israel's life as a reflection of Israel's unhappy experiences with her own kings. As such it is said to have very little value as a historical source for the reconstruction of events at the time of the establishment of the monarchy. More recently A. Weiser has defended the notion that I Sam. 8 is rooted in old traditions which record opposition to the monarchy at the time it began. He is followed in this by a number of scholars.[35] He still reads the chapter as distinctly anti-monarchical in tone. Scholars are generally agreed that in its present position chapter 8 is intended to attribute the introduction of kingship which follows as due to the demand of the people. They agree that the figure of Samuel is given special prominence here, and that he is portrayed as only reluctantly complying to the people's demand.

I Sam. 8 has generally been considered to be a literary unit, but a close examination of the chapter indicates some signs that the literary history of this chapter is more complex than most would claim. Several matters point to an earlier level of tradition which stands somewhat in tension with the final form of the chapter. In the early verses of the chapter the request for a king is clearly motivated by the breakdown in the administration of justice due to the corruption of Samuel's sons. Although the phrase ככל-הגוים appears in vs. 5 it receives no comment at all in Samuel's reply, yet in the latter half of the chapter (esp. vss. 8ff.) the issue centers on the tendency of the people to adopt foreign practices and the danger that brings. The people's request for a king is now seen as motivated by the desire to adopt foreign ways. There seems to be a clear conflict between vss. 7b and 8b in the matter of

Samuel's position before the people. In 7b Samuel is assured
that the people's action is not directed at him but at God
(כי לא אתך מאסו); however, 8b seems to say just the opposite.
God tells Samuel that the people are acting toward him also in
forsaking their God (כן המה עשים גם-לך). Three times in the
chapter (vss. 7, 9, 22) God commands Samuel to listen to the
people, and the last time he tells Samuel to "make them a king"
(והמלכת להם מלך). The first time (vs. 7) God seems to be
soothing Samuel's displeasure in the previous verse, and in vs.
9 his only condition to the kingship is that the people be
warned of the משפט המלך. This reiteration of God's acquies-
cence in the people's request would seem to stand in tension to
the harsher statements in vs. 8 where their request is equated
with past forsaking of God (עזב) and in vs. 18 where it is implied that the people run the risk of complete abandonment by
Yahweh. To be sure, these points do not constitute exception-
ally strong evidence on which to base any hypothesis, but in
light of the increasing tendency of scholars to argue that
chapter 8 must be based on old tradition,[36] these points might
at least lend support to the hypothesis that fragments of that
old tradition can still be seen in the chapter. Further support can be seen only after more thorough analysis. It at
least seems clear that the chapter is not the smoothly unified
composition of a single hand.

At this point rather than proceeding straightforwardly
through the chapter as it now stands it would perhaps be more
profitable to raise the question concerning the extent of the
Deuteronomistic material in the chapter. There can be little
doubt that Deuteronomistic language and influence are actually
present in the chapter. There are several points at which this
is most evident. The vocabulary of vs. 8 seems clearly Deuteronomistic. The term אלהים אחרים used with either הלך אחרי or
עבד is a typical Deuteronomic phrase. It appears eighteen
times in the Pentateuch only three of which are outside Deuteronomy.[37] W. Richter has demonstrated that the use of the verb
עזב should also be considered Deuteronomistic.[38] It appears in
a Deuteronomistic context in Jdgs. 2:12, 13; 10:6, 10, 13; Jos.
24:16, 10; I Sam. 12:10 where it is also connected with the

verb עבד. The identification in vs. 8 of Israel's chief sin as
that of continued apostasy is a well-known theme both in Deuteronomy and in the Deuteronomistic introductions in the Book
of Judges. Vs. 18 is also to be reckoned to a Deuteronomistic
hand. Here the verb זעק is being used in the manner of Judges
10:10, 12 as the cry from an oppressed people, repentant and
expectant of God's delivery. Thus, vss. 8 and 18 have the effect of interpreting the request for a king in a manner similar
to the Deuteronomistic view of the period of the judges. The
request for a king runs the risk of renewing the cycle of sin,
oppression and cry for help once again, but it is implied in
vs. 18 that deliverance might not follow this time. The use of
the phrase ככל-הגוים in vss. 5 and 20 has often been cited as
Deuteronomistic, and there is little reason to dispute this
claim. The only parallel to the phrase occurs in the law of
the king in Deut. 7:14ff. where the concern is to guard against
the adoption of foreign practices by the king while reluctantly
allowing the kingship itself to exist. At this point it is
clear to see that all of the passages which can be most easily
identified as Deuteronomistic have in common the view of the
kingship as an institution which runs the risk of leading Israel into forsaking God by the adoption of foreign gods and
customs.

The passage in vss. 11-18 seems somewhat different than
the rest of the chapter in form. Its formal structure seems to
mark it as a stereotyped description of the burden a king may
be expected to place on his people in the fulfillment of the
material needs of a royal court.[39]

Generally this picture is considered to be a late reflection of Israel's experience with her own kings. However,
Mendelsohn, using data from Ugarit and Alalakh, has demonstrated that the picture could just as well be of the common practice of Canaanite kings as early as the thirteenth century.[40]
This would increase the likelihood that what is intended here
is a description of the excesses of pagan kingship. Such excesses in terms of material gain are precisely forbidden the
Israelite king in the law of the king in Deut. 17:14ff. It is
thus more likely that vss. 11-18 refer to this repugnance

toward foreign practices rather than Israel's own experience
with kings. This would be consistent with the concerns of the
Deuteronomistic writer in vs. 8. H. Seebass[41] has again noted
that the term משפט המלך in 8:9 and the term משפט המלכה in 10:25
are strikingly similar. Scholars have generally regarded it as
likely that the two terms are related. Yet, as the text now
stands they refer to extremely different things. The reference
in 10:25 speaks of a legal document of some sort which clari-
fies the basis of kingship at the time of Saul's accession.
However, in its present context, 8:9 seems to refer to the description of vss. 11-17. If the two phrases are related then
we have an unnecessary double announcement of the משפט המלך.
10:25 is a clear statement that this was a legal document.
Certainly 8:11-17 does not seem to be such a document. Its
connection would seem closer to the concern to guard Israel
from foreign influences we have noticed in the Deuteronomistic
passages (e.g. vss. 8, 18). It seems unlikely then that 8:9
(משפט המלך) and 10:25 (משפט המלכה) are from the same hand. Despite the apparent relation between the two phrases, it is
clear they are used in totally different ways. Even the En-
glish RSV translation makes it obvious how difficult it is to
construe the two references in the same manner.[42] Vs. 18 in
its use of the temporal formula ביום ההוא (2x) shows clearly
that its prediction that the people will cry out for help is
contingent on the description in vss. 11-17 actually coming to
pass. This tie to vs. 18 makes it seem likely that the Deuteronomist is responsible for the insertion of these verses although they bear no evidence of having been composed by him.
They would fit well with the Deuteronomistic conern to guard
against pagan influences (a concern also expressed in vs. 8 and
the use of ככל-הגוים in vss. 5 and 20). Thus far it may be
said that there is clear evidence of a Deuteronomistic hand in
the chapter, although the exact extent of his influence is
still unclear, and that this same hand is probably responsible
for the use of the stereotyped description in vss. 11-17.

An important question to be raised at this point is whether or not the whole chapter should be considered Deuteronomistic. The clearest evidence that it is not can be found by

comparing chapter 8 with chapter 12. As we shall see more
fully at a later point, I Sam. 12 represents perhaps the most
clearly Deuteronomistic composition in the entire block of material I Sam. 7-15. Chapter 12 shows clear knowledge of the
tradition of the people's demand since 12:12b seems to reflect
8:19. But 12:12 places this demand in the context of the
threat from Nahash the Ammonite. This is an entirely different
setting than that of chapter 8 where Samuel is growing old and
his sons are inadequate to succeed him. If 12:12 represents
the Deuteronomistic tradition then it seems unlikely that the
whole of chapter 8 can be considered Deuteronomistic. The Deuteronomistic editor may well have added his material as a supplement to an older tradition, a method he is known to have
used elsewhere.

It must now be asked where it is possible to detect elements of older tradition in the chapter. Little discussion is
required in regard to I Sam. 8:1-2, for most scholars are
agreed that this notice must stem from a genuine old tradition
which recorded the names of Samuel's sons and the fact that
they were judges in Beer-sheba.[43] The location of Samuel's
sons in Beer-sheba certainly stresses his widespread influence.[44] In its present position I Sam. 8:1-2 serves both as a
continuation of the theme of Samuel as the administrator of
justice in 7:16-17 and as an introduction to the need for a
king to aid in the administration of justice. In fact, it is
extremely difficult to divide vss. 1-2 from what follows and
claim as some do that the Deuteronomistic work begins in vs. 3.
In the present literary structure of the chapter vs. 3 is obviously connected with both the tradition of Samuel's sons
which precedes it and the request of the elders which follows.
This is seen most clearly by the similar phrases ולא הלכו בניו
בדרכו in vs. 3 and ובניך לא הלכו בדרכיך in vs. 5. The issue
over which the need for a king arose is here clearly identified as the administration of justice. Samuel's age and the
corruption of his sons render the present system unworkable.[45]
The purpose of the king according to the elders is to render
justice (לשפטנו, vs. 5; cf. also vs. 20). Samuel is displeased,
but the point of his displeasure is that the people said

תנה-לנו מלך לשפטנו not that they wanted to be like the nations
(ככל-הגוים). This is remarkable in light of the strong emphasis elsewhere in the chapter on the temptation to adopt foreign
ways and gods which the kingship presents. The early portion
of the chapter seems to see the demand for a king as a potential threat to Yahweh's kingship, but Yahweh still instructs
Samuel to listen to the people. This might be called a "sinful-
but-still-of-God" view of the kingship. It appears to be the
clearly Deuteronomistic portions of the chapter (vss. 8ff.)
that add to this the note of foreign practices that might be
introduced through the kingship and relates this to Israel's
continued apostasy with foreign gods (vs. 8). In any case
there is no reason to exclude the "sinful-but-still-of-God"
view from the older tradition. It may well reflect an authentic, early tradition rooting in circles that felt a tension between the traditions of the league and the institution of kingship, as Weiser and others have suggested.[46]

Surely it is apparent that we have in chapter 8 an old
tradition recording the request of the people for a king due to
the breakdown in the administration of justice. This old tradition has been overlaid and reworked by the Deuteronomistic
writer with an emphasis on the dangers inherent in the kingship
and on the connection of this request to the people's constant
tendency to forsake their God.[47] The older tradition material
can best be detected in the earlier part of the chapter (vss.
1-7) while the influence of the Deuteronomist's work dominates
the remainder of the chapter (vss. 8ff.). In the early part of
the chapter the Deuteronomist's influence can be seen only in
his possible addition of the final phrase in vs. 5. That it is
an addition can be seen by the fact that Samuel's reply takes
no account of it whatsoever. We would attribute vs. 7 to the
older tradition because of its essential conflict with vs. 8 in
the matter of Samuel. God tells him that he is not rejected in
vs. 7, but in vs. 8 says that the people have forsaken him.
Further, although not a decisive point, it is interesting that
vs. 7 uses the word מאס for the turning of the people from God
while vs. 8 uses עזב. We have already seen עזב to be typically
Deuteronomistic in usage, but while מאס appears thirty times in

the prophetic books and five times in the Pentateuch none are
in clearly identifiable Deuteronomic or Deuteronomistic contexts. Vs. 8 raises the issue of Israel's continued sin which
is well known in Deuteronomistic contexts and relates it to the
request for a king. The theme of Yahweh's theocratic rule in
vs. 7 was formerly thought to be of late development, but more
recent scholarship has shown this concept to be at least as
early as the period of the tribal league and its appearance in
vs. 7 need not influence our attribution of this verse to the
earlier tradition. [48] Vss. 19-22 may also have some connection
to earlier tradition. Vs. 7 seems to be re-echoed in vs. 22,
and vs. 20 is reminiscent of vs. 5b (although with an interesting shift of ככל-הגוים to the prime position). To conclude
these remarks it is necessary to emphasize that an attempt to
divide completely the Deuteronomistic work from the earlier
tradition which he used is probably doomed to failure since his
work seems to have overlaid the latter portion of the old account entirely. However, we do believe that it is possible to
detect the general outline of the old tradition in vss. 1-7,
and that it is therefore possible to contrast the viewpoints of
the old tradition and the later Deuteronomistic hand on the
people's request for a king.

* * *

To summarize briefly our results:
A. An old tradition concerning the request of the people
of Israel for a king can be seen in vss. 1-7. There is little
reason to doubt that this tradition is rooted in the genuine
historical memory of an active role by the representatives of
the people in the establishment of kingship. This tradition
views the request for a king as motivated by the perversion of
justice, and there is no sign that this is considered to be a
poor reason. The tradition makes quite clear that Yahweh allowed the establishment of the kingship despite Samuel's displeasure. This might be called a "sinful-but-still-of-God"
view of the kingship, which is less harsh than the Deuteronomistic view seen elsewhere in the chapter.
B. The present shape of the chapter is due to the hand of
the Deuteronomistic writer who edited the chapter extensively

in order to interpret the people's request as raising the danger of apostasy. His influence can be seen most clearly in vss. 8 and 18, in the phrase כל-הגוים in vss. 5 and 20 and in the use of the stereotyped description in vss. 11-17. The description of vss. 11-17 is of pagan kingship similar to that which is prohibited in Deuteronomy 17:14ff., and if this type of king rules over Israel there will be no help available from Yahweh. The Deuteronomistic writer views the kingship here as a distinct danger in tempting the people to apostasy, although there is no evidence that he tried to cover over the tradition that Yahweh allowed the kingship to be established.

I Samuel 9:1-10:16

There is remarkable agreement among the majority of scholars who have worked on I Samuel that the pericope in 9:1-10:16 of the young Saul searching for the lost asses and being confronted with his own anointment by Samuel belongs to the so-called early source.[49] Many of these same scholars agree that this early source also includes I Sam. 11 and most of 13-14 which together with 9:1-10:16 form a history of the rise of Saul. Some scholars have, however, stressed that this is a rather loose collection of materials with considerable differences in style and viewpoint.[50] There is also a general consensus on the general character of 9:1-10:16. Since Gressmann[51] most scholars have concurred in the opinion that the pericope is marked by folkloristic elements, and the corollary has been that it is therefore unreliable for use in historical reconstruction. In common with the rest of the early source and in contrast to the so-called late source (7, 8, 10:17ff., 12) the pericope is said to exhibit a positive attitude toward Saul and the monarchy in general. The unity of the pericope itself has not often been challenged, but recently several scholars have suggested that 9:1-10:16 shows evidence of a prior reworking. Hertzberg[52] suggests that there are two originally independent sources here but concludes that they cannot now be separated. In any case it was the combined account that was incorporated into the larger framework of the history of the rise of Saul and later into the Book of I Samuel as we now

have it. Seebass[53] also believes that there are two independent traditions present in the section and attempts a complete
spearation of the two. However, in doing so he is forced to a
minute division of materials that stretches the limits of cre-
dibility. We shall have occasion to look at some of his suggestions in greater detail below. In general it might be said
that although scholars have recognized some tensions within
9:1-10:16 the tendency has been to treat the section as a unity
in discussing the literary analysis of I Samuel.

We have already implied that the question of whether or
not 9:1-10:16 should be considered to be a literary unity must
be answered in the negative. A careful reading of the text
discloses a number of tensions and inconsistencies in the pericope:

1. Vss. 9:6-8, 10 refer to a 'man of God' residing at a
far off city who is apparently unknown to Saul. In 9:9, 11-13
this same figure is referred to by the term 'seer', ראה, and is
still an unknown local figure. However, from 9:14 on this
figure becomes Samuel, who has the authority from God to anoint
Saul as נגיד over Israel and who is seemingly well known (10:
14-16). This Samuel seems similar to the important leader of
Israel seen in I Sam. 7-8, but the local man of God/seer certainly does not.

2. In 9:19a Saul is told by Samuel to go up to the high
place before him while in 9:22 Samuel himself escorts Saul and
his servant to the place where the meal is to take place.

3. Samuel promises in 9:19b to inform Saul concerning
everything that is on his mind the following morning. Immediately, however, in 9:20 he tells Saul that the lost asses have
been found. This makes 9:20 a doublet of 10:2 which accords
much more closely to the promise in 9:19b.

4. In 10:1 (reading with the LXX) reference is made to a
single sign, האות, whereas in 10:7, 9 the reference is in the
plural, האתות.

5. It is strange that while Samuel apparently predicts
several signs in 10:2-8 only the fulfillment of the last one is
narrated (10:10).

Besides these tensions within the pericope we might also
mention that there is at least one clear example of an

explanatory editorial insertion in 9:9. Further, 10:5 and 8
show editorial attempts to link this pericope to chapter 13.
It has always been held, however, that these verses are late
insertions into the already complete pericope and hence, tell
us nothing about the development of the chapter. Certainly we
can conclude at this point that the evidence shows that 9:1-
10:16 cannot be considered to be a literary unity without some
adequate explanation of the tensions within the section. Any
reconstruction of the growth of the section into its present
form will first require a careful examination of the character
and origin of the various materials in the section.

Even a cursory reading makes clear that 9:1-2 is an introductory formula designed to give us pertinent information on
the principle figure in the action which follows. The more
common formula for giving information in introducing a main
character actually begins with the name of the character followed by his father's name, his tribe or home or both, any special information which is necessary, and a transition to the
action of the narrative. Examples of this formula may be found
in Jdgs. 3:15; I Sam. 17:12; I Kgs. 11:26. As can be seen
there is some flexibility to the order of the elements in the
formula. The type of formula used in 9:1 is similar but somewhat more dramatic since the chief figure is named last and it
begins on a more flourishing note with the construction ויהי
איש.[54] An example of this formula in its most skeletal form
can be seen in Jdgs. 17:1 where the order is ויהי איש, tribe or
home, and name followed by a statement of the occasion for the
narrative usually introduced by waw consecutive. I Sam. 9:1-2
represents an imaginatively expanded form of the formula since
it adds a genealogy and special information after the name. It
is also interesting that the writer has made Kish the subject
of the introductory formula whereas Saul, his son, is actually
the principle figure in the following narrative. Saul is introduced in the special information about Kish, and we are even
given additional information on the unusual physical beauty of
Saul. This has the effect of interrupting the normal transition into the action of the narrative (introduced by waw consecutive at the start of vs. 3) by a centering on the person of

Saul, and it thus makes clear at the start that the ultimate
focus of the narrative is Saul himself rather than the seemingly commonplace search for lost animals with which the story begins. It should also be noted that this notice on Saul's physical appearance is reminiscent of the ideal picture given of
others whom tradition has cast in the heroic mold or destined
for a special career (Joseph, Gen. 39:6; David, I Sam. 16:12,
18; 17:42; Absalom, II Sam. 14:25). This focus on the ideal
picture of Saul and the distinctly dramatic style of the introduction seem to indicate that 9:1-2 is of a piece with the
folkloristic account of Saul's search for the lost asses which
follows in 9:3ff.

We have already had occasion to note that it was Gressmann
who first popularized the view that the story of Saul's search
for the lost asses in 9:3ff. bears the characteristic features
of the folk tale (Märchen).[55] Among these features Gressmann
lists the following:

1. The fanciful theme--how Saul, as a young man, went to
search for lost asses and found a kingdom!

2. The ideal picture of a young man who excels all others
in stature and appearance.

3. The namelessness of the city to which Saul and his
servant come and the namelessness of the seer who dwells there.

4. The indefiniteness of time.

5. The entire atmosphere of the story which moves in the
realm of wonders rather than fact.

The relegation of 9:1-10:16 to the category of the folk tale
has led many scholars to dismiss the entire section in a manner
similar to Lods when he describes it as "undoubtedly at bottom
only one of these political legends with which popular fancy
loves to invest the beginnings of great men."[56] Certainly it
is undeniable that folkloristic elements appear in the section,
but is this characteristic of 9:1-10:16 as a whole? Most of
Gressmann's features hold true for the early part of the chapter but in 9:13 the nameless seer is identified as Samuel; in
vs. 9:20 a specific temporal statement is made; and the revelation of Yahweh to Samuel concerning a commission to be given
Saul for the delivery of Israel (9:15ff.) seems to strike a

theological note reminiscent of prophetic themes rather than
the wonderous themes of folk tales. The possibility must be
considered that not all of 9:1-10:16 is to be included in the
folkloristic theme of Saul's search for the lost asses. Let us
ask first which portions of the section can be clearly attributed to the folk tale tradition of Saul's youth.

There can be little doubt that 9:1-13 belongs to the folk
tale. All of Gressmann's features listed above can be found
here. Further the style itself in these verses seems suited to
the rendering of a delightful story. It is unhurried yet vivid
and charming. Information is given to the reader by means of
conversations between the characters. There is time for a
building of tension in 9:4 through the repetition of the statement that the asses were not to be found after each successive
journey through a strange land in search of them. There is
also time for the device of a conversation with the young maidens as a way of conveying the information about the sacrifice
and the coming meal. The picture of Saul here is that of a
rather inexperienced young man who is forced to rely on his
servant for guidance. There is little reason to doubt the
usual conclusion that 9:1-13 is simply the beginning of a
charming folk story about the young Saul.[57] Vs. 9:9 clearly
represents a parenthetical note probably inserted into the text
by a later hand. We will comment further on the purpose of
this note at a later point in this chapter.[58]

Now we may ask what portions of the entire section clearly
belong with 9:1-13. It is apparent that the two encounters
Samuel predicts for Saul in 10:2-4 must be included with the
original folk tale tradition. 10:2 is paralleled by 9:5. Saul
is concerned in 9:5 that his father's worry over the lost asses
would give way to concern for the welfare of his son, and in
virtually identical language 10:2 reports that the men Saul is
to encounter will tell him that this has indeed happened. In
Saul's second encounter (10:3-4) the men are to give him bread,
and this would seem to be related to the fact that in 9:7 Saul
tells his servant that their bread is completely gone. It
could also be noted that in 10:2-4 the reader is again in the
realm of wonders.

The special meal in 9:22-24 must also belong with 9:1-13. The maidens to whom Saul speaks as he approaches the city reveal that after the sacrifice on the high place there will be a meal to which only those who are invited will come (9:13). Hence, it is truly wondrous when Saul and his servant, who have just come to the city as strangers, are not only invited but given a place of honor.[59]

It would seem likely that 9:18-19 are also to go with the folk tale of Saul's youth. In vs. 19 we find the actual invitation by Samuel to Saul to join the meal on the high place. Here also is the promise to tell Saul all that is on his mind. The only matters with which we have reason to believe Saul was concerned are the lost asses and the lack of provisions. Vss. 10:2-4 then represent the fulfillment of Samuel's promise. In the morning Samuel relieves Saul of concern for both the lost asses and the lack of bread. Some have seen a discrepancy between Samuel's command to precede him to the high place in 9:19 and the indication that Samuel was actually escorting Saul and his servant in 9:22. This conflict is more apparent than real since 9:22 says nothing of the passage up to the high place but refers to Samuel's escort of Saul and his servant into the banquet hall. There is no conflict between 9:18-19 and 9:22-24.

We have thus been led to the conclusion that the folkloristic tradition of Saul's search for the lost asses must have included at least 9:1-13, 18-19, 22-24; 10:2-4. One major problem remains: the unknown seer of 9:1-13 is clearly identified as Samuel in 9:18-19, 22-24. Can these then belong to the same original tradition? The seer is first identified as Samuel in 9:14, and we did not include that verse with 9:1-13 precisely because we had not yet discussed this problem even though vs. 14 forms the natural conclusion to the section. If we may be allowed to be a bit speculative for a moment, let us assume that the revelation to Saul of the seer's identity as Samuel is precisely one of the dramatic high points of the story. It is impossible to argue that the materials which mention Samuel by name are from a different source since we have already seen the number of intimate connections between some of these materials. It would be in keeping with the dramatic

flair of the tale if the author intended to give the impression
that Saul was seeking out a local seer for advice when, much to
the surprise and delight of the reader (or listener?), as Saul
is entering the city it is Samuel who comes out to meet him.
Vs. 18 shows that Saul does not recognize him, but he is only
a youth.   Vs. 19 confirms for the reader that indeed the seer
whom Saul sought was the famous Samuel, for Samuel himself
states "I am the seer." This interpretation gains support when
we look more closely at the syntax of 9:14. The mention of
Samuel by name is preceded by the exclamatory particle
which serves to emphasize the subject (Samuel) which follows as
if it were unusual or unexpected. A further bit of evidence
might be seen in the closing phrase of 9:24 ויאכל שאול עם-שמואל
ביום ההוא. We already know that they ate together. The only
purpose for this note must be that the author wished to emphasize this point. This, in fact, must be one of the main points
of the original folk story: Saul, as a young man, actually encountered Samuel before Saul himself had any notion of his future destiny, and amazingly, Samuel not only invited him to
dine but made him the honored guest and foretold the finding of
the asses and the replenishing of supplies. To the hearer such
a story must surely have shown that even as a youth Saul was
destined for special things, although he himself did not real-
ize it at the time.

Much of the material in 9:1-10:16 which remains as yet un-
discussed cannot be appropriated to the old folk tale tradition
we have been tracing. This material displays a formal structure of a radically different nature and is thereby marked as
stemming from a completely different setting than the folk tradition. N. Habel,[60] by examining the calls of Moses, Gideon
and a number of the classical prophets, has concluded that
there is a formal literary structure which characterizes call
narratives. We believe that in I Sam. 9:15ff. is a modified
version of this same form. Habel lists the major divisions of
the call narrative as follows: 1. divine confrontation, 2. introductory word, 3. commission, 4. objection, 5. reassurance,
6. sign.[61] All of these elements are present in the Samuel/
Saul account but in an altered order: 1. divine confrontation,

2. introductory word, 3. objection, 4. commission, 5. sign.,
6. reassurance. A closer examination of each element will make
clear the need for some of these modifications.

1. The Divine Confrontation, 9:15 - This element is not
greatly elaborated but simply states that a divine confrontation took place. This is similar to the call of Gideon and in
contrast to the more elaborate visionary elements of the confrontation in the calls of Moses and Isaiah. In contrast to
Gideon, however, is the fact that Yahweh himself is the agent
of confrontation. The idiom גלה את-אזן also emphasizes the
direct character of the confrontation which is more characteristic of the prophetic calls than that of Gideon. Already in
the first element of the form one of the major differences between the usual call narrative and our modified form is apparent. There are two principals involved. Saul's call and commissioning is seen as mediated through God's prophetic agent,
Samuel. This presence of a prophet as a mediating figure is
reminiscent of Elijah in I Kgs. 19:15-16 where God commands him
to anoint Elisha as his successor, thus making Elijah the agent
of Elisha's prophetic call. Interestingly, the same passage
contains the command to anoint Jehu as king. Samuel's role is
thus quite similar to that of Elijah. However, since the account is couched in the call-form it probably finds its setting
in a period somewhat nearer the beginning of the activity of
the writing prophets.

2. The Introductory Word, 9:16-17 - Habel has identified
the function of this element to be "to spell out the specific
basis or grounds for the commission."[62] This preparatory word
will vary with the historical situation. Here as in the usual
call narrative the situation necessitating the commission is
clear; Yahweh is responding to the Philistine domination by
calling forth a deliverer. Yahweh himself reveals the urgency
of the crisis in words similar to the call of Moses (Ex. 3:7,
9) ראיתי את-עני-עמי כי באה צעקתו אלי.[63] Here the introductory
word also serves to identify the recipient of the commission,
a variation made necessary by the two-character modification of
the form. Hence, in vs. 16 Saul is identified preliminarily
as a Benjaminite who will arrive at a given time, and in vs. 17

when he actually arrives Yahweh himself indicates that he is
the man. The introductory word in 9:16-17 also serves to anti-
cipate the actual commissioning in 10:1. In fact, almost the
entire commission can be paralleled in the introductory word.[64]

10:1	משחך יהוה לנגיד על-עמו על-ישראל	9:16	ומשחתו לנגיד על-עמי ישראל
10:1	ואתה תעצר בעם יהוה	9:17	זה יעצר בעמי
10:1	ואתה הושיעתו מיד איביו מסביב	9:16	והושיע את-עמי מיד פלשתים

This thorough anticipation of the commissioning of Saul lessens
the significance of the fact that the objection precedes the
actual commissioning in our modified form. In a sense the commission has already been made by Yahweh. Saul has been singled
out by Yahweh for the delivery of Israel, and 10:1 represents
the delivery of this commission to Saul. For Habel the verb
שלח is of key importance in the commission,[65] and yet שלח appears in our section only in 9:16. Thus, it is underscored
that in some sense Saul is already sent of Yahweh before his
actual commissioning in 10:1.

   3. The Objection, 9:21 - Because the actual commission
does not come until 10:1 the author is forced to give some
foreshadowing of it to Saul in vs. 20b or the objection would
have no reference. Vs. 20b then hints at a special mission for
Saul without giving any of the specifics of its nature. It
should also be noted that vs. 20a serves to remove the lost
asses as the main item of attention in the story. This is done,
however, at the cost of consistency with the promise to tell
Saul of them in the morning (vs. 19). The objection itself is
similar to that of Gideon in Jdgs. 6:15. In contrast to God's
choice of them to deliver his people Gideon and Saul both claim
to be from the least of tribes and families (cf. also Ex. 3:11;
4:10; Jer. 1:6). Because of the reversal in elements in the
form of the Samuel/Saul call narrative the objection of Saul
has a slightly different force than that of Gideon. Gideon's
objection is that he is inadequate to the task, but since Saul
has not yet been commissioned his objection must be taken to
mean that he feels unworthy of the choice itself.

   4. The Commission, 10:1 - The commission of Saul is preceded in 9:27 by the significant notice that this is to be

considered as a revealing of the Word of God (ואשמיעך את-דבר
אלהים). This again shows the influence on the form of the
presence of a prophetic mediator as the agent of the call to
Saul. It probably also reinforces the hypothesis that the setting for this tradition of Saul's call to save Israel is to be
found in prophetic circles. The commission itself begins with
a rhetorical question. As with Gideon (Jdgs. 6:14) the question re-emphasizes the divine origin of the commission. The
actual content of the commission is found in the direct commands. Like Gideon, Saul is called to save Israel; hence, he
is God's agent just as are the prophets, although they are
called upon to announce God's word.[66] Indeed, Saul's commission is the Word of God made known to him via God's prophet
Samuel (9:27).

There is a further and more important difference between
the commission of Saul and that of Gideon. Saul's commission
is accompanied by an act; he is anointed (משח).[67] This anointing is performed by God's prophet and by it Saul becomes נגיד
over Israel.[68] The role of the prophet in designating kings is
attested in the period of the divided kingdom. Elijah is told
to anoint Jehu (I Kgs. 19:15-16) although Elisha actually carries this out (II Kgs. 9). Ahijah, the Shilonite, designates
Jeroboam as king (I Kgs. 11:29ff.), but without reference to
anointing. Ahijah does, however, refer to this designation of
Jeroboam as making him נגיד (I Kgs. 14:7). Certainly in 10:1
this anointing is to be taken as the climactic point of the
narrative as it now stands. Everything before was pointed
toward it, and everything which comes after is to confirm its
significance. It is interesting that Saul is not anointed as
king which might be expected. This surely indicates that the
editor who was responsible for the inclusion of Saul's call
and commission knew of the accounts of how Saul became king and
that it was not his intention to give us another version. His
concern was merely to show that before Saul actually assumed
the kingship he was designated by Yahweh to deliver Israel and
anointed by Samuel. This concern may have dictated the use of
the term נגיד as well. Its roots probably lay in northern and
possibly in tribal league tradition (see n. 68) and it would

thus commend itself for use at this point by the editor since
he knew Saul was not yet king.

It is important to note that the anointing is said to be
from Yahweh. This is in contrast to the demand of the people
for a king in chapter 8. It is interesting there that although
the people's request for a king is heeded they have no role in
the making of a king. Yahweh gives this task to Samuel (8:22).
It would seem to be the concern of the editor to emphasize Yahweh's ultimate authority in this matter mediated by his prophets. We might also mention at this point that it is part of
our hypothesis that the career of Saul as Yahweh's anointed one
forms one of the central unifying themes to a pre-Deuteronomistic, prophetic redaction of these materials. This discussion
must, however, be left to a later point.

5. The Sign, 10:1, 5-7a - The first mention of a sign
comes in 10:1b (LXX) before the word of reassurance. It is in
the singular (האות) and must refer back to the commission itself. Saul is commanded to save Israel from the hand of her
enemies, and the fact that he will do this is the sign that
Yahweh has chosen him. His anointing is thus to be vindicated
by his deeds in delivering Israel, an important theme in the
development of later material. However, according to Habel,[69]
the sign normally belongs not with the commission but with the
reassurance in order to give additional confirmation of the
presence of God with the one who has been called. The next
reference to a sign is in 10:7a where the word is plural
(האותות). The usual interpretation has been to take this as a
reference to vss. 2-6; thus there are three signs. We have already seen, however, that the two predictions of 10:2-4 can be
connected closely with the folk tradition of the lost asses.
Vs. 5 divides itself off from the material which precedes it by
the use of אחר כן which emphasizes the distinction that is to
be made between the previous predictions and that which follows. Vs. 7a refers back to only vss. 5-6; Saul will come to
Gibeath-elohim; he will be met by a band of prophets; the
spirit of Yahweh will come upon him; and he too will prophesy.
These events constitute the 'signs.'[70] Such a view gains support from a closer look at the section 10:5-8. Scholars have

often singled out vss. 5a and 8 as later redactional insertions
since they seem to refer to 13:3 and 8. It is true that these
verses seem clearly to refer to chapter 13, but this need not
imply they are insertions. Vss. 10:5-8 might be from an editorial hand which, we will argue, has been influential in
bringing much of the Saul tradition together. The section then
becomes not only the conclusion of the call narrative but the
foreshadowing of those future events which the editor feels to
be of greatest importance in the account of Saul. Upon meeting
a band of prophets Saul is to receive the spirit of Yahweh (10:
10-13). Once he has received the spirit Saul is to "do what-
ever your hand finds to do" (עשה לך אשר תמצא ידך), for God is
with him. As some have suggested this could well be a reference to chapter 11.[71] Finally the reference to the sacrifices
at Gilgal and the seven-day wait clearly refer to the first
story of Saul's rejection (13:8) which represents the demise of
Saul as God's anointed. The prophetic editor is making clear
that one of his organizing principles is Saul's career as God's
anointed. Returning to the element of the sign in the call
schema one can now suggest that there may not be a reversal of
the reassurance and the sign elements of the form. Vs. 7a only
predicts the sign; its actual fulfillment comes in 10ff.

    6. The Reassurance, 10:7b - We have already noted the
formula כי האלהים עמך in vs. 7 as the reassurance. It differs
from the usual formula by being in the third rather than the
first person, but again this is due to the presence in our account of Samuel as an intermediary figure.

    All of the elements of the call narrative as outlined by
Habel are present, and the permutations of the form are easily
understandable. They stem from the presence of Samuel as an
intermediary figure necessary for the anointing of Saul, and
from the desire of the editor to place this in the context of
an earlier folkloristic account of a meeting between Samuel and
Saul. The existence of an independent tradition of an encounter between Samuel and Saul served to make believable the editor's assertion that a secret anointing had taken place. We
have already suggested that the setting from which this editorial work stems is to be found in prophetic circles concerned

to posit a prophetic anointing of Saul leading to his posses-
ion by the spirit.

We have not discussed 10:10-13 except to suggest that this
is the fulfillment of the promised sign in the call schema. We
would now suggest that the editor had at hand for this purpose
an old and independent tradition of Saul's prophesying. However, the purpose of this old tradition was aetiological since
it served to explain the origin of the evidently common proverb
in 10:11, 12. Another version of the origin of this proverb is
found in 19:18ff. In any case it is clear that the original
function of the tradition was to explain the saying. The editor has simply used this tradition by having Samuel predict
such an occurrence in 10:5-6 thus incorporating it into his
call schema as the sign, and the original meaning of the saying
here becomes secondary to Saul's actual prophesying. Other
evidence that vss. 10-13 must have originally been independent
of vss. 5-6 may be seen in the difference in divine names. Vs.
6 uses Yahweh while in the same phrase vs. 10 uses Elohim. The
place names in vss. 5 and 10 are also slightly different.

10:14-16 has not yet been mentioned, and although it
raises many questions most must remain unanswered. Suddenly
with no transition whatsoever Saul is talking to his uncle in
vs. 14. Why his uncle? Where is he? There is no information
to aid us here.[72] It seems most likely that this is a part of
the original conclusion to the folk tale since it resumes the
theme of the lost asses. The insertion of other material into
the folk tale has not left this conclusion intact. Vs. 16b
must be redactional. The major problem with this half verse is
the use of the word 'kingdom' המלוכה when in fact Samuel did
not use royal language in the preceding section. It may be,
however, that the editor considered the ultimate point of
Saul's anointment to be his rise to kingship and has simply
anticipated himself. In that case 16b could be attributed to
the prophetic editor who is here reinforcing the secret nature
of the anointing. This emphasis on secrecy explains why this
event was not known to the people before.

* * *

42

To summarize our findings:

A. An old folk tale beginning with Saul's search for the lost asses may be found in 9:1-14, 18-19, 22-24; 10:2-4, 9, 14-16a. The theme of this tale was Saul's unwitting encounter as a youth with Samuel. Saul ate with him as the honored guest and was relieved by the foretelling of the solution to the problems of the lost asses and the depleted bread supplies.

B. An old aetiology of a popular proverb is to be found in 10:10-13. As an explanation of the saying it records a tradition of Saul's prophesying with a band of ecstatic prophets.

C. An editor has taken the folk tale as the context for the insertion of a tradition of Saul's anointing by Samuel since the folk tale recorded an early meeting between the two before Saul was king. This insertion possesses the formal structure of a prophetic call narrative although it has been modified to allow for a mediating role by Samuel and to allow for the fact that it is being worked into another tradition. For the fulfillment of the sign element in his schema this editor has used the old aetiological tradition in 10:10-13. The use of the call narrative form gives us a clear indication that this editorial work was carried out in circles influenced by prophetic tradition. The role of Samuel is clearly that of the prophetic designator of kings and is in keeping with the picture of early prophetic activity found elsewhere. The work of the editor may be seen in 9:15-17, 20-21, (25-26), 27-10:1(LXX), 5-8, 16b. Central in this editor's concerns are the prophetic role of Samuel as God's agent in designating and anointing Saul, God's initiative in the choice of Saul, the prophetic anointing as the source of Saul's authority and the possession of the spirit which follows this anointing. The attitude toward Saul is positive although the focus seems to be more on God's calling of Saul than on Saul himself. He is important as God's anointed.

I Samuel 10:17-27

Most scholars who have advanced critical theories for the composition of the Books of Samuel have reckoned this section to the late source.[73] As such it is said to continue the anti-monarchical tone claimed for I Samuel 7 and 8. Most would see I Sam. 10:17ff. as the direct literary continuation of chapter 8, the two having been separated by the editor who intertwined the early and late sources. The late source is continued from 10:17-27 in chapter 12. Martin Noth attributes this section to the Deuteronomistic historian, but not without qualifications.[74] Although he believes the section, especially in its first part, to have been formulated by the Deuteronomist, he states that it appears to play no essential role in the thought patterns of the Deuteronomist. Further, he agrees that 10:21bβ-27a apparently represents an old tradition telling of Saul's choice for king arising out of his physical stature. O. Eissfeldt was the first to advance this theory that 10:21bβ-27a could be divided off from the story of Saul's choice by lot.[75] Noth makes clear, however, that he does not regard this as an independent narrative thread, but that it is a tradition fragment so completely assimilated by the Deuteronomist that the two cannot be separated literarily. Noth is then able to conclude that the present form of the tradition is due entirely to the influence of the Deuteronomist, and agreeing with those who place the section in the late source, he also finds the section to be distinctly anti-monarchical in tone.

There is little new that can be said about 10:17-27 from a literary-critical viewpoint. A minor observation can be made about vs. 27b. Here the phrase ויהי כמחריש has long been recognized as a particularly awkward continuation of vs. 27a.[76] Many scholars, on the basis of the LXX reading, have emended this to read ויהי כמחדש. This is a slight emendation and the construction using the inseparable preposition כ with the preposition מן in a temporal construction is found also in Gen. 38:24 (ויהי כמשלש חדשים). The emended reading fits perfectly as an introduction to chapter 11 and as a transition from 10: 27a, and we will here accept the emendation.

The major literary-critical observation to be made in this section has already been made by Eissfeldt.[77] He argued that a seam in the narrative can be found between vss. 21bα and 21bβ. The narrative as it now stands represents the combination of two originally independent traditions. According to one the

choice of the king is determined by the sacred lot. Tribes,
families and men are taken by lot until finally Saul is designated. The other tradition records that Saul is indicated as
the one whom God had chosen by his impressive stature in comparison with the rest of the people. To this tradition belongs
the incident of Saul's hiding among the baggage.[78] Although
some have argued against this division[79] there are strong arguments in its favor. The chief evidence is an understanding of
the sacred lots. J. Lindblom, in a thorough study of lot-
casting in the Old Testament, has pointed out that the evidence
indicates that the lot could answer only yes or no or give no
answer at all.[80] Thus, it is highly unlikely that one who was
not present could be chosen by the lot as the present text
seems to indicate. Further the revelation from Yahweh that one
was hiding in the baggage could not be given by the lot but
represents some type of oracular designation. The question in
vs. 22 according to the MT makes little sense if Saul has already been chosen ("Is there yet a man to come here?" עוד הבא
איש הלם), but if 21bβff. is taken as an originally independent
tradition the implication is that no suitable candidate for the
kingship is found and the inquiry of Yahweh becomes necessary.
Yahweh then reveals that there is one who has not been considered hiding among the baggage, and when he is found his stature
clearly indicates him as the man Yahweh has chosen. Thus, on
close examination one can concur with Eissfeldt that two originally independent traditions are probably present here although
it seems impossible completely to separate them literarily.
However, we have already noted that many scholars agree that a
fragment of old tradition is present in the narrative as we now
have it. The greatest division of opinion concerns the nature
of the context in which this tradition is found and the role
this old tradition now plays in that context. To answer these
questions, however, requires a closer examination of all of the
materials in 10:17-27.

We have already established that our section contains two
versions of Saul's designation as king, and the nature of each
deserves a closer examination. The actual narrative of the
choice by lot stands in vss. 20-21bα.[81] Its formal style

corresponds exactly to the account of the designation by lots
of Achan as the violator of the holy ban in Jos. 7:14-18. In
both accounts we are dealing with a stylized description of the
lot-casting procedure. The presentation of each tribe, family
or individual to the decision of the lot is described through
the use of the verb קרב, and the designation of one of the
parties is described by the use of the verb לכד. One who is
not so designated is said to 'go out', יצא (cf. I Sam. 14:41).
In vs. 21 one should probably read with the LXX the clause that
indicates that the family of the Matrites was brought near man
by man since the MT as it now stands accords well with neither
the procedure of lot-casting nor the narrative description of
this procedure as it appears in Jos. 7:14-18. There is little
reason to doubt that 10:20-21bα represents a genuinely old
piece of tradition cast in the formal style customary for the
narrative description of a lot-casting. The mention of Saul's
family as that of Matri, המטרי, is a piece of information not
given to us elsewhere and adds weight to the conclusion that
this is a fragment of genuinely old tradition.

The second tradition on the choice of Saul lies in 10:
21bβ-24. In its present form this tradition lacks a beginning,
for it opens with the question "Is there a man yet to come
here?" This would indicate that the tradition originally included some account of an attempt to find a king-designate
which ends in failure. It might even be speculated that this
original beginning was a lot-casting and that the difference
between the two traditions really lies in the outcome of the
lot-casting procedure. In any case, this second tradition records that Saul was finally designated not by lot but by an
oracle of Yahweh which revealed that he was hidden among the
baggage. In 10:23 Saul is found and proves to be taller than
any of the people. This is the same motif as was encountered
in 9:2 although there Saul was also claimed to be more handsome
than all the people. The motif of Saul's stature in vs. 23 is
not, however, merely an attempt at editorial harmonization with
9:2. Both are probably founded in a common tradition of Saul's
stature which some would claim is based in historical fact.[82]
However, in 10:23 the motif has become significant in direct

relationship to Saul's elevation to the kingship. Vs. 24 emphasizes that it is Yahweh who has chosen Saul, and his stature
in vs. 23 acts as a prior sign attesting to this divine choice.
In no way is it suggested that it is because of Saul's stature
that he becomes king. The divine choice has already been made,
and it is now being revealed to the people. C. J. Labuschagne
has noted that central to the speech of Samuel in vs. 24 is the
claim of incomparability.[83] The use of the construction of
comparative negation (אין כ...) is the most common means of expressing incomparability: There is none like X. It is significant that the immediate preface to Saul's acclamation as king
by the people is a formal statement of incomparability (כי אין
כמהו בכל העם) closely linked to a designation of Saul as the
chosen one of Yahweh. Most commentators have related the
statement of incomparability back to the fact of Saul's stature
mentioned in vs. 23, but the speech of Samuel does not refer to
this as a basis for the claim of incomparability. Saul's stature is but a sign; it is the divine election that singles him
out from the people as king. This divine election is the focus
of the tradition. Yahweh has chosen a king completely apart
from the normal means of cultic designation which have apparently failed. Labuschagne's study indicates that the formula
of incomparability is used to claim uniqueness and to exclude
all rivals who might claim the throne. "We may even suppose
that this particular pronouncement by Samuel became a standard
formula used at the coronation ceremonies of the Israelite
kings. This, however, cannot be proved, but there are definite
reminiscences of the phrase in I Kgs. 3:12, 13 and Neh. 13:26
(referring to Solomon), in II Kgs. 18:5 (referring to Hezekiah)
and in II Kgs. 23:25 (referring to Josiah)...For our purpose
it is of importance to note that the newly-elected king is
called incomparable, because only he, to the exclusion of all
others, has a claim to the throne."[84] He is the elected of
Yahweh. The acclamation of the people (יחי המלך) represents
their recognition and acceptance of God's choice. The same
formula appears elsewhere as an expression of recognition connected with accession to the throne, II Sam. 16:16; I Kgs. 1:
25; II Kgs. 11:12. Here too, we may be dealing with a formula

proclamation from the coronation ritual itself, but the evidence
is insufficient to be certain. In any case, the emphasis of
the tradition is clearly on the extraordinary election of Saul
by Yahweh, a choice which the people witness by their acclamation. There are certainly no pejorative implications directed
against kingship here.

It would seem that the two traditions of the choosing of
Saul as king were joined literarily. Certainly vs. 21bβ has
been made to read as if the person who could not be found was
Saul who was just taken by lot, although we have already seen
the impossibility of such an event. It is impossible, however,
to tell whether this half verse was an original part of the
second tradition or a transitional clause composed by an editorial hand. That there was an editorial hand is made clear by
the insertion of the adverb עוד in vs. 22 in recognition of the
presence of two separate procedures. We would assume that the
phrase וישאלו-עוד ביהוה belongs to the tradition in vss. 21bβff.
and that its scope has been expanded by the adverb to harmonize
the two traditions.

It is vss. 17-19 which introduce the section 10:17-27 that
are most often claimed to show Deuteronomistic influence and
yet it is difficult to find any clear evidence of such influence. There is one clear parallel to I Sam. 10:17-19 in Jdgs.
6:7-10, and W. Richter has pointed out the extensive verbal
parallels that may be drawn between the two:[85]

I Sam. 10:17-19		Jdgs. 6:7-10	
17	צעק	7	זעק
	אל-יהוה		אל-יהוה
18	ויאמר	8	ויאמר
	כה אמר יהוה אלהי ישראל		כה אמר יהוה אלהי ישראל
	אנכי העליתי את-ישראל ממצרים		אנכי העליתי אתכם ממצרים
	ואצל אתכם מיד מצרים	9	ואצל אתכם מיד מצרים
	ומיד כל הממלכות הלחצים אתכם		מיד כל-לחציכם

Richter also detects a Deuteronomistic hand in Jdgs. 6:7-10 and
lists the evidences he finds there of that hand, but it is precisely these elements that are missing in I Sam. 10:17-19. "Zu
DtrG oder seiner Umwelt würde am ehesten verweisen: V. 7; V. 8

48

V. 10 אגרש;‏ V. 9 אוציא אתכם מבית עבדים;‏ אורציא אתכם מפניכם;‏ איש נביא‏
Die Synopse zeigt, ‏...ולא שמעתם בקולי;‏ לא תיראו את-אלהי האמרי‏
dass die Wendungen, für die Dtr vermutet würde, nicht in I Sam.
10:17-19 stehen."[86] One can only conclude that while both passages seem to show a reliance on the same independent formulaic
elements[87] the Jdgs. 6 passage shows clear evidence of a Deuteronomistic hand while I Sam. 10:17-19 does not. It is worth
noting that there are no points of comparison at all between
the later portions of both passages (I Sam. 10:19; Jdgs. 6:9b-
10). It is here that both passages direct their common material toward different ends, and it is here that the Deuteronomistic material in the Jdgs. 6 passage becomes most predomi-
nant.

We have been looking only at certain formulaic elements in
10:17-19, but there is also a distinct formal structure to
these verses which may be profitably analyzed. This formal
structure may be schematized in the following manner:

Call to Assembly, vs. 17 - As in chapter 7 it is Samuel
who calls the assembly together, and the gathering place is
Mizpah. The assembly in 10:17 is cultic ('before the Lord')
and thus sets the stage for the Yahweh speech which is to follow.

Messenger Formula, vs. 18aα - It is stated clearly here
that Samuel addresses the people, yet what follows is the messenger formula and a first person speech from Yahweh. From
this there can be little doubt that Samuel appears here as a
prophet and that the speech itself seems to be following prophetic forms of address. Certainly the very full form of the
messenger formula here (כה-אמר יהוה אלהי ישראל) has long been
identified as one of the standard hallmarks of prophetic
speech.[88] God's word is being directed to his people by means
of the prophetic messenger, Samuel.

Recitation of Saving Acts, vs. 18aβb - Here we have the
direct first person address as if Yahweh himself were speaking.
This first person quality receives additional force by the emphatic use of the independent pronoun אנכי. Thus the going up
from Egypt and the delivery from enemies are not in themselves
the focus of this recitation. It is the fact that these things

came about solely through the agency of Yahweh ("*I* brought up Israel..."). Basically this historical recitation is an expansion of the accusation in the standard prophetic judgment speech against the nation. It provides a background to the accusation. Westermann notes that "this is generally the most important and most frequent expansion of the judgment against the nation and it is found in all the writing prophets from Amos to Ezekiel: Hos. 9:10-13 and ch. 11 in each stanza; Isa. 5:1-7, Jer. 2:1-13, Micah 6:1-4... It is the only expansion that is already found in the early form of the judgment against an individual as a reminder of the saving acts that God had manifested to the king."[89] It is interesting to note that the similar recitation in Jdgs. 6:8b-9a is exactly the same as that in 10:18 until the final portion where 10:18 adds the word הממלכות instead of simply using the plural participle of לחץ. This addition attracts special attention because it is a feminine plural noun used in connection with the masculine plural participle הלחצים. It seems likely that הממלכות is an insertion into a standard recitation formula, perhaps added to give irony to the people's request for a king by pointing out that it was nations with kings who were Israel's oppressors.

Accusation, vs. 19a - The accusation of the people is introduced by the emphatic use of the independent pronoun אתם. The focus of the speech has shifted to the actions of the people in contrast to those of Yahweh, thus creating a syntactically dramatic tension between these two parts of the speech (*I*...but *you*...). At first glance this contrast of God's deeds to the offense of the people seems to be similar to Amos 2:9-12, which W. H. Schmidt has argued is Deuteronomistic,[90] and to some of the prose materials in Jeremiah which are often cited as Deuteronomistically influenced (Jer. 7:22-26; 34:13-14). A closer examination, however, reveals an important difference. I Sam. 10:17-19 uses Yahweh's saving acts as a contrast to the present sin of the people (note the use of היום in vs. 19). Amos 2:12, however, is clearly contrasting Yahweh's saving acts in the past to Israel's *past* rejection of Yahweh which has continued into the present. The same is true of the contrast drawn in Jer. 7:22-26; 34:13-14. Although different in form

LIBRARY
McCORMICK THEOLOGICAL SEMINARY
1100 EAST 55th STREET
CHICAGO, ILLINOIS 60615

the Amos passage is closer to the theme of I Sam. 8:8 where
stress is placed on the *continual* sin of Israel. Westermann
has noted that this difference in the use of the recitation of
God's acts as an expansion of the accusation seems to reflect
the general development of the form. "At the first it is an
expansion containing only a contrast: God's kind deed in the
past is contrasted to the offense of the addressee... A further step can already be seen, however, in Amos 2:12; joined to
the kind deed of God is Israel's reaction to it in the past."[91]
Certainly it is the latter pattern which is best known to us
from Deuteronomy and later Deuteronomistic materials. The request of the people for a king is equated in I Sam. 10:19 with
rejection of Yahweh, and the people's reasons for such a request are here left undefined. This half verse is clearly related to 8:7 where the motif of the rejection (מאס) of God appears. The verb מאס does not appear in a clearly Deuteronomistic context but is common in the accusations of prophetic oracles of judgment (Amos 2:4; Hos. 4:6; Isa. 5:24; 8:6; Jer.
6:19; 8:9). The rejection-of-God motif is an expression of the
people's resistance to God's directing will and implies nothing
of the worship-of-foreign-gods motif common to Deuteronomistic
materials (cf. 8:8). Our study of chapter 8 showed that the
rejection-of-God motif in 8:7 could well belong to the old tradition, and its presence in 10:19 does not indicate Deuteronomistic influence.

Announcement, vs. 19b - In the most common form of the
prophetic speech one would expect to find here an announcement
of judgment growing out of the accusation made in vs. 19a, but
as Westermann has pointed out the announcement can carry elements other than judgment.[92] This is the case in 10:19b. The
announcement is introduced dramatically by the particle ועתה
which indicates that what follows is to resolve the dramatic
tension set up in the previous two parts of the speech. However, when we look at what follows in vs. 19b we are disap-
pointed, for it is a somewhat bland imperative commanding the
people to present themselves before Yahweh. What has happened
to the conflict between God's saving will and Israel's apparent
rejection of that will? To answer that question the reader

must broaden his viewpoint. The effect of the command in vs. 19b is to form a direct transition to what follows so that the entire narrative in vss. 20ff. is taken into the announcement as the resolution to the tension between God's acts and the people's rebellion. We have already seen that in its present form the narrative in vss. 20-24 places a strong emphasis on the action of Yahweh in choosing Saul as king. Thus, the divine response to the people's rejection is strikingly to reassert the divine will through the very institution which the people chose as the focus of their rebellion, the kingship. The people do not force the choosing of a king; God's choice had already been made and is only now revealed to the people. Indeed, the present position of 10:17ff. after the account of the anointing of Saul in 9:1-10:16 serves to emphasize the fact that God's will had preceded and anticipated the rebellious will of the people. There is indeed a judgment implied in vs. 19a, but it is against the people and not the kingship. In effect, 10:17-27 takes the theme of the people's rejection of Yahweh and redeems it. In the old tradition seen in 8:1-7 the kingship was viewed as "sinful-but-still-of-God." In 10:17-27 the people have rebelled, but God's choice of a king has anticipated that as the placing of 9:1-10:16 is intended to show. Certainly the extremely positive view of the king in 10:20ff. does not allow us to see the section as lacking in enthusiasm for the kingship itself. There can be little doubt that the formal structure of 10:17-19 as we have described it stems from earlier prophetic rather than Deuteronomistic circles. It is possible that a similar prophetic formal pattern lies behind Jdgs. 6:7-10 although its present form clearly shows Deuteronomistic influence. We do have material showing some knowledge of the old tradition in chapter 8, but there are no ties to clearly Deuteronomistic material there. More than likely a later hand knowing the old tradition of the people's rejection of God seen in 8:1-7 has reappropriated it so as not to reflect badly on the kingship itself, but this was clearly prior to the Deuteronomistic writer.

The use of the term משפט המלכה in 10:25 has been often cited as a parallel to משפט מלך in 8:9. Although the terms are

similar we have already seen in the analysis of chapter 8 that
they appear in totally different contexts for totally different
purposes. It is clear that 10:25 indicates a written, legal
document placed in the sanctuary whereas 8:9 is a verbal warning given by Samuel at public assembly. In the absence of
other clearly Deuteronomistic influences in 10:17-27 the similarity of the two phrases in 8:9 and 10:25 would constitute
rather slim evidence for arguing that 10:17ff. relates to the
Deuteronomistic portions of chapter 8.

The dismissal of the people in 10:25b seems like a natural
conclusion to the pericope, and the continuation in vss. 26-27a
seems somewhat awkward. It certainly is not essential to the
preceding material. On the other hand, these verses contain
some interesting material which must root in genuinely old traditions. In vs. 26 we find that men of might (בני החיל LXX)
attach themselves to Saul. It is likely that this reflects the
beginnings of a small standing army under Saul. A similar tradition is found in 14:52. The mention of opposition to Saul by
some "worthless men" (בני בליעל) probably roots in the existence of some genuine resentment or skepticism toward Saul in
the early days of his kingship. Having noted that genuine elements of old tradition may lie here, we can observe that vss.
26-27a have been intentionally composed as a transition section. The next section of material is the account of Saul's
victory over the Ammonites in chapter 11. There Saul is sum-
moned from the fields of his home in Gibeah, and 10:26 admirably sets the stage by giving us a clear notification of Saul's
return to Gibeah. Further in vs. 27 the focus of opposition to
Saul is whether or not he can function as a deliverer, a question admirably answered in chapter 11. Vs. 27 should also be
seen as the prerequisite for understanding the incident recorded in 11:12-13 which we shall discuss at a later point. An
editorial hand has clearly made 10:26-27a a transition to the
following pericope. Clear evidence as to the identity of this
editor is lacking, but a clue might lie in the fact that according to vs. 26 it was God who drew men of might to Saul.
This is in distinct contrast to 14:52 where it is Saul himself
who attaches men to his band, but it is quite in keeping with

the thorough emphasis on the centrality of God's activity in
10:17-25. Thus, we might tentatively conclude that vss. 26-27a
stem from the same hand which shaped the rest of the pericope.
It might be mentioned that the mere application of the term
בני בליעל to Saul's opponents shows that the writer was well-
disposed toward Saul.

* * *

To summarize our conclusions on 10:17-27a:

A. Two originally independent traditions relating how
Saul was chosen as king are to be found in 10:20-24. The seam
between the two lies in vs. 21bβ, but a separation of the two
leaves them both incomplete. They have probably been combined
prior to their inclusion in the present context. Both show the
choice of Saul as one made by God although the emphasis on this
is much stronger in the tradition of Saul's designation by divine oracle and his subsequent acclamation by the people.
There is no hint of a negative view toward Saul or the kingship.

B. The rest of the pericope (10:17-19, 25-27a) shows the
presence of a hand which has been influenced (particularly in
vss. 17-19) by prophetic forms of speech. It clearly portrays
Samuel as a prophet proclaiming an oracle of judgment against
Israel, but the accusation is followed not by an announcement
of judgment but by God's act of grace in choosing a king for
Israel. Samuel is the prophetic agent through whom God has already designated Saul in 10:1, and now Samuel is God's agent
in Saul's public presentation. The editor has introduced the
old traditions of the choice of Saul with a prophetic speech
and followed them by the promulgation of the משפט המלכה. He
has evidently made use of some fragments of old traditions in
vss. 26-27a although the present literary form of these verses
is probably due to his hand. The complete pericope evidences
a strong concern to emphasize the initiative of God in the
choice of Saul (similar to the anointing in 9:1-10:16). Although there is judgment implied against the people in vs. 19a
the response is a reassertion of the divine will in the kingship itself, a turn of events which can hardly be considered

anti-monarchical and might well be considered a clarification of the old tradition in 8:1-7 with its "sinful-but-still-of-God" view of kingship. There is no detectable Deuteronomistic influence in the pericope.

I Samuel 11

For those who have defended a two-source theory for the First Book of Samuel, the account of Saul's victory over the Ammonites has, since Wellhausen[93] and Budde,[94] been unanimously attributed to the early source. This conclusion has not been entirely without qualifications, especially among more recent scholars. Most, although agreeing that the Ammonite victory tradition belongs to the early source, would want to see all or part of 11:12-14 as a redactional addition, thus limiting the old tradition to 11:1-11, 15. However, these scholars are divided on the relationship of 11:1-11, 15 to other material usually attributed to the early source (9:1-10:16; 13-14). Some would argue for a close connection of ch. 11 to 9:1-10:16 usually on the basis of the common motif of spirit possession.[95] These scholars see 9:1-10:16 and 11:1-11, 15 as integral parts of a single literary source positive to Saul and the monarchy. Others prefer to place the stress on the original independence of the two traditions in 9:1-10:16 and 11:1-11, 15. A few have postulated that these materials represent two distinct literary sources.[96] Others claim they represent traditions preserved at different cult centers or simply in different geographic locales (Jabesh/Gilgal; Ramah/Gilgal).[97] Still others simply stress the independent origins of the two sections by pointing out the completely different character of each (most often legendary vs. historical).[98] However, despite these minor differences most of those stressing the original independence of chapter 11 from 9:1ff. would still claim that they came together in a pro-monarchical history of the rise of Saul which was later edited together with an anti-monarchical strand of tradition. This makes the connection of chapter 11 to other materials secondary but in the end returns to the two-source theory. In the final analysis scholars are generally agreed that I Sam. 11 is perhaps the most reliable historical tradition in the

materials on the rise of kingship in Israel, and that its viewpoint is positive to Saul and to the monarchy. They also point
out the minor role of Samuel here and stress the fact that even
his limited appearance is mostly confined to vss. 12-14 where
most see the influence of an editorial hand.[99]

A careful reading of I Sam. 11 does uncover some literary
basis for asking whether or not the work of an editorial hand
can be detected here. In vs. 7 the phrase "and after Samuel"
ואחר שמואל raises suspicion when it is noticed that apart from
this phrase Samuel plays no role whatsoever in the delivery of
Jabesh-Gilead from the Ammonites. Yet, the implication is that
both Samuel and Saul will lead the people. As has been previously suggested by many scholars, the phrase is probably to be
regarded as secondary. This suggestion is supported by the
fact that the preposition אחרי is used for Saul while in a sup-
posedly parallel phrase the preposition אחר is used for Samuel.

The notice concerning the thirty thousand men of Judah in
vs. 8b is also strange. In the muster of the levy in vs. 7 it
was only necessary to note that messengers were sent through
the territory of Israel, surely denoting the entire tribal
league. It would seem odd that the number of men from one
tribe should be specially noted apart from the number who came
from the rest of Israel. Again we may probably identify the
Judah notice in vs. 8b as a secondary addition to the text. In
this case we are given a clue to the time of this editor since
it is unlikely that such a separation of Judah from Israel
would date before the division of the kingdoms when Israel and
Judah became distinct entities.

The notice of an attempt to put to death some of those who
opposed Saul appears abruptly in vss. 12-13. Vs. 11 ends the
battle account with a suitable closing formula, and with no
transition at all the people seem to be assembled to pose a
life and death question before Samuel. The notice ends just as
abruptly with a statement by Saul, and we are still left won-
dering who these men were whose lives have been spared. In any
case the cryptic nature of the notice and the fact that it
bears little relation to what precedes or follows it provide
ample reason to give 11:12-13 a closer examination below.

Vs. 14 has been almost universally claimed as redactional although there is less agreement on the identity of the redactor. It has long been recognized that the exhortation of Samuel 'to renew the kingdom' נחדש שם המלוכה at Gilgal stands in contradiction to vs. 15 which indicates that it was on this occasion at Gilgal that Saul was actually 'made king' וימלכו שם שם-שאול by the people. This discrepancy must be taken into account in any attempt to treat the development of I Sam. 7-12.

It is clear that an editorial hand has been at work, and it is probable that chapter 11 plays some role in a larger editorial scheme. To discern this we must turn first to a discussion of the nature of the traditions to be found in chapter 11 and the uses to which they have been put.

In the narrative of Saul's delivery of Jabesh-Gilead in 11:1-11, it is clear that the picture drawn of Saul is that of the charismatic hero such as appears in the Book of Judges. This narrative is, in fact, the only clear instance of the muster of the tribal levy outside of the Book of Judges.[100] As in chapter 7 we are again dealing with more than an old battle account, for the form and language is that of holy war. The theme is deliverance as is shown in vss. 3 and 9 (מושיע, תשועה), but although the actions of Saul seem to occupy the foreground the deliverance is regarded as from Yahweh (vs. 13 עשה-יהוה תשועה בישראל); it is the 'spirit of God' רוח-אלהים (vs. 6) that comes upon Saul and it is the 'dread of Yahweh' פחד-יהוה (vs. 7) that falls upon the people to bring them out. Richter has pointed out that I Sam. 11:1-11 is a good example of a second type of holy war schema.[101] We have already noted the first type in chapter 7 where the victory is attributed more directly to Yahweh who strikes the enemy with panic.[102] Here the holy war schema is connected with the rise of a deliverer who acts as God's agent in the battle. The various elements of this type of holy war schema are also found in Jdgs. 3 and 6. Richter stresses, however, that in I Sam. 11 the holy war schema is the framework around which the narrative is constructed whereas in Jdgs. 3 and 6 the elements of the schema are scattered through a narrative showing other interests than that of holy war.[103] The formal elements of the schema may be described as follows:

Identification of the situation and the enemy, vss. 1-4 (cf. Jdgs. 6:33) - While a brief notice of the Ammonite siege of Jabesh would have sufficed the author is here (and as we shall see throughout) concerned not with giving a report but with telling a good story. He paints a brief picture of the enemy whose unusually harsh terms and attitude of contempt accentuate his role as the villain. The theme of "Who will save us?" is struck at the beginning (vs. 4).[104]

Possession of the spirit, vs. 6 - The motivation of God's spirit (רוח) is also recorded for Gideon (Jdgs. 6:34) and Jephthah (11:29; 13:25). The use of the verb צלח is used in connection with spirit possession only for Samson (Jdgs. 14:6, 19; 15:14), earlier for Saul (10:6, 10), and in a clearly late passage for David (16:13). It is clear that in 11:6 the possession of the spirit becomes the motivation for all that follows: hence, the impetus is God's. Here, as also in Jdgs. 14: 19, the possession of the spirit is clearly distinguished from the anger with which Saul responds.

Mustering of the tribal levy, vss. 7-8 - Elsewhere this element is accompanied by the 'blowing of the horn' (Jdgs. 3: 27; 6:34; I Sam. 13:3), but this motif is missing here. The author does record the cutting up of oxen whose pieces are then sent throughout the tribes accompanied by a conditional curse directed at those who do not respond to the summons. A parallel to this bizarre summons is found in Jdgs. 19:29ff., and the tradition may have its roots in ancient practice. Jdgs. 21:5 would seem to indicate that the summons to avenge the death of the Levite's concubine was also accompanied by a curse against those who did not respond. The author of I Sam. 11:1ff. is concerned here to show that even the people's response is at the initiative of Yahweh since it is following the falling of the פחד-יהוה that the people come forth "as one man," כאיש-אחד. The numbers are reported and then the author turns from the holy war schema momentarily in order to build dramatic tension in vss. 9-10. Having received the message of imminent aid the men of Jabesh give an answer to the Ammonites to which the author has intended a double meaning in anticipation of the coming victory.[105]

Account of the victory and notice of complete annihila-
tion, vs. 11 - There is a brief deployment notice relating that
Saul divided his men into three companies (as Gideon, Jdgs. 7:
16) and that the attack was at the morning watch (similar to
Ex. 14:24). The whole schema is then concluded with one of the
formulae of annihilation typical of holy war accounts, ולא
נשארו-בם שנים יחד (cf. Ex. 14:28; Jdgs. 4:16).

There can be little doubt that the narrative of 11:1-11 has
been influenced in its formation by the schema of holy war described above. Most scholars have felt this narrative to represent a genuinely old tradition which may be taken in sub-
stance as historically authentic although embellished by the
tendency of the author to interpret the victory as achieved by
one inspired with the divine charisma. The conclusion that
this is old and reliable tradition is supported by references
elsewhere to the close relationship between Jabesh-Gilead and
the tribe of Benjamin and Saul in particular. Judges 19-21 records the fact that Jabesh-Gilead did not participate in the
punishment of Benjamin and thereby incurred penalty against
herself.[106] In I Sam. 31:11ff. and II Sam. 2:4bff. it is the
men of Jabesh-Gilead who risk their lives to recover Saul's
body from the Philistines and give it honorable burial.

Is the narrative of 11:1-11 related originally to 9:1-
10:16? Probably not, in the light of our analysis of these
sections. Although both might be said to stress the activity
of God in events surrounding the rise of the kingship the expression of this activity takes quite different forms. There
is nothing in 11:1ff. of the prophetic influence we detected
in the final shaping of 9:1-10:16, and the figure of Samuel
plays no significant role in 11:1-11 (perhaps none at all).
It is the common motif of the possession by the spirit in 10:6,
10 and 11:6 that has led to the confusion. Eissfeldt, for instance, has felt it necessary to regard 11:6a as an intrusion
from another source (J).[107] There is a similarity of language
in the use of the verb צלח, but the operation of the spirit is
completely different, one displaying the group ecstasy of the
prophetic schools and the other calling forth the individual

acts of the charismatic hero. It may be that Saul was known as
a man of the spirit in both senses since both 10:10 and 11:6
are located in old traditions. The reference in 10:6, however,
we have seen to be a later editorial piece, and it may well be
that the common motif of the spirit of God has served to influence the secondary relationship of 9:1-10:16 in the present arrangement of materials in I Samuel. We shall return to this
question later.

Vs. 15 has generally been regarded as belonging originally
with the narrative of the delivery of Jabesh in vss. 1-11.
Following Saul's victory over the Ammonites, the people assembled at Gilgal make him king and celebrate his accession with
sacrifices and feasting. This account then becomes a parallel
version of Saul's rise to the kingship in 10:20-24.[108] It is
significant that 11:15, in contrast to the prophetically influenced material on Saul's rise to the kingship, stresses that it
is the people who make him king. R. Knierim[109] has argued that
the early kings took office by the commission of the people and
that the prophetic materials which stress the role of Yahweh in
choosing and commissioning a king represent a systematic reinterpretation of the tradition. David was anointed king by the
people in II Sam. 2:4; 5:3, and it is only in a later prophetically influenced tradition in 16:13 that an anointment from
Yahweh via his prophet is encountered.[110] Knierim feels the
same may have been true of Saul since the LXX reads καὶ ἔχρισεν
Σαμουὴλ ἐκεῖ τὸν Σαοὺλ εἰς βασιλέα. He interprets this as indicating that Saul was originally anointed on the authority of
the people and not of Yahweh, but the reappearance of Samuel in
the LXX version makes this hypothesis difficult. Knierim is
forced to assume that Samuel is acting here as the agent of the
people. In any case, the MT is quite clear that Saul is made
king by the people, and this may relate to the request of the
elders in chapter 8 which is probably based in old tradition
although now reworked by a later prophetic hand. Despite the
difficulties in using the LXX reading, Knierim's general point
may be well-founded that later reinterpretation of the traditions to emphasize the role of Yahweh in the choice of Saul has
taken place. However, the evidence remains slim, and the

hypothesis must be considered somewhat speculative. We would
still tentatively conclude that I Sam. 11:15 represents an old
tradition showing Saul's accession to the kingship on the initiative of the people. This version has been preserved despite
the tendency of surrounding material to emphasize the role of
Yahweh in choosing Saul and the role of Samuel as Yahweh's
agent in this choice (cf. also 12:1 where Samuel claims to have
made the king; this will be treated at a later point).

The tradition of the people's initiative in making Saul
king in vs. 15 has definitely been weakened by Samuel's statement in vs. 14, "Come, let us go to Gilgal and there renew
(חדש) the kingship." Most scholars have regarded this verse as
the clearest evidence of redactional activity in this chapter,
and there would seem to be little reason for challenging this
conclusion. A. L. Merrill[111] has argued that the verse is
original on the basis of his claim that the root, חדש, is not
here to be read as "renew." He notes Ps. 51:12; 104:30 as instances where it stands parallel to ברא but then strangely sees
its usage in 11:14 as covenantal, meaning "fulfill" in the
sense of bringing to fruition. It is doubtful, however, that
these arguments seriously challenge the translation of חדש in
11:14 as "to renew." The parallels to ברא can be accounted for
by simply noting that renewal can easily be seen as carrying
overtones of new creation motifs. It would seem clear that an
editor has, in the process of ordering the traditions as we now
have them, attempted to harmonize an apparent duplication.
Saul has already become king in 10:24 so the instance in 11:15
has been transformed into a renewal. It is interesting to note
that it is the account stressing the people's action which has
been played down. As a renewal their action serves only to
confirm a choice actually made previously by God himself and
proclaimed through his prophet, Samuel. It is interesting that
Samuel appears again in 11:14 as the one who identifies the
ceremony as a renewal.

The interesting tradition on the sparing of Saul's opponents in vss. 12-13 has been taken by most as redactional and
belonging with vs. 14. This is usually done on the basis of
the seeming lack of connection with any surrounding material

and the common claim that the men involved are those mentioned
previously in 10:27a. We can agree that these verses do not
seem of a piece with 11:1-11, 15, but this need not mean that
it is a complete editorial composition. More likely it is a
piece of old tradition placed here for a particular purpose by
a later hand. In general, commentators have failed to deal
adequately with the meaning of this small fragment of tradition. Almost uniformly it is interpreted as a witness to the
magnanimity of the deliverer, Saul, and a disapproving word
directed toward those who are motivated by vengeance. However,
since 11:12-13 must surely be related to the opposition against
Saul recorded in 10:27a,[112] a close study of the tradition
shows such a view to be based mainly on sentiment.[113]
R. Knierim has emphasized that the matter is one of sacral justice, not of vengeance and mercy. "The request of the people
for the punishment of Saul's slanderers is not at all an act
of 'petty vengeance.' It is a necessity of sacral justice...
After Saul's victory, it was proven by divine judgment that the
despisers had not merely slandered Saul but also Yahweh's mes-
siah, and with that Yahweh himself... The desire of the people
...is a legitimate and necessary demand to execute judgment
against the convicted slanderers of Yahweh."[114] In 10:27a
these opponents of Saul are already called בני בליעל. In the
Old Testament the איש בליעל is one who slanders God or breaks
sacral law (I Sam. 1:16; 2:12; Jdgs. 20:13; 19:22; Nahum 1:11;
Deut. 13), destroys justice (I Kgs. 20:10; Prov. 19:28), destroys life (Prov. 16:27), or rebels against the king (II Sam.
16:7; 20:1; 23:7; Job 34:18); and all of these acts call for
the judgment of death. The text itself is quite clear that
Saul did not pardon these opponents because he was feeling
generous. He states in apodictic form, "No man shall be put to
death on this day," לא-יומת איש ביום הזה, because God has delivered Israel. A legal pronouncement is made on the basis of
God's act of salvation and not because of Saul's magnanimity.
What is significant about this is the apparent transfer to Saul
of the right to make judgments in the sacral/legal realm. It
is significant that in vs. 12 the people approach Samuel with
the matter, but in vs. 13 it is Saul who deals with the question. It is natural that Samuel as the judge of Israel and

62

authority in such matters should be approached, but it is clear
that the outcome shows Saul in the position to act authorita-
tively on the matter. It should be pointed out that this small
fragment of tradition serves to set up the later situation of
Saul's rejection precisely because of his lack of concern for
matters of sacral law. There, as we shall see, it is Samuel
as prophet who acts as the upholder of God's law in confronting
Saul with his violations. The earlier materials in 10:25 and
11:12-13 make clear that Saul is charged with responsibilities
in the sacral/legal realm.

It is clear from the above discussion that editorial activity in chapter 11 is not extensive, but this should not be
taken to mean that the chapter plays no significant role in a
larger editorial context. The insertion of Samuel in vs. 7,
the concern for sacral justice in vss. 12-13, and the reduction
of the notice that the people made Saul king to a renewal of a
previous choice of Saul by God are all matters that accord well
with the general concerns of the prophetic editor whose influence we have traced in earlier material. It seems not unlikely
then that he has been responsible for the placement of this
chapter in its present relationship with preceding materials.
As such the chapter plays an important role as the public functioning of the charisma which Saul possesses as a result of his
anointing and subsequent possession by the spirit. It has long
been recognized that the claim of a divine vocation is thought
in some strata of the Old Testament to be verified by the public functioning of the charisma bestowed by the call to vocation.[115] We believe this to be one of the organizing concerns
of the prophetic editor in tracing the career of God's anointed. David, too, is anointed, possessed by the spirit, and then
demonstrates his charisma publicly in the defeat of Goliath.
It would seem clear that chapter 11 has been placed in its
present position in order to serve a definite purpose in the
later prophetic editor's treatment of Saul's career as God's
anointed.

* * *

Our results may be briefly summarized as follows:
A. I Sam. 11:1-11, 15 is an originally independent tradition picturing Saul as a charismatic hero similar to those

found in the Book of Judges. The whole account is structured around the framework of a holy war schema, but it concludes by the people's elevation of Saul to the kingship seemingly on the basis of his victory. It is probably to be regarded as an old tradition with some basis in actual fact since we know elsewhere of the close relationship between Jabesh-Gilead and Saul. One should, nevertheless, exercise caution in using this tradition as the basis for a historical reconstruction of the period.

B. This old tradition has been incorporated by a later editor into a larger context. He has anticipated it in 10:7 and introduced it with the skepticism of Saul's opponents in 10:27a. This theme of Saul's opponents, which is probably an old tradition which the editor has simply used, is taken up again in vss. 12-13 in order to show the shift of the responsibility of sacral justice to Saul. The hand of the editor may also be seen in additions in vss. 7 and 8b and in the interpretation of the coronation in vs. 15 as a renewal by the insertion of vs. 14. This serves to maintain the primacy of God's choice of Saul.

I Samuel 12

For scholars who hold to a two- or three-source theory for the composition of the Books of Samuel, chapter 12 has always been considered one of the focal points for the late source which is also found in I Sam. 7; 8; 10:17ff.[116] However, most of these scholars have also detected traces of Deuteronomistic influence in the chapter and have claimed that the material has undergone a later redaction at the hands of Deuteronomistic editors. They differ on the extent of this redactional activity. Martin Noth has popularized the view that the whole of chapter 12 can be attributed to the work of a Deuteronomistic historian whose hand is strongly in evidence in the other materials usually attributed to the late source in I Samuel.[117] For Noth, I Sam. 12 is one of those key passages which stand at the turning points in the Deuteronomistic history and serve to tie it together.[118] Where possible, these take the form of speeches by major figures in the history (Jos. 1:11-15; Jos.

23; I Sam. 12; I Kgs. 8:14-61), but sometimes the writer is
forced simply to offer his reflections (Jos. 12; Jdgs. 2:11-23;
II Kgs. 17:7-23).[119] These constitute something of a theological meditation on Israel's history at each crucial point. Many
scholars who are not willing to see the Deuteronomist as responsible for other materials attributed to the late source do
agree that a Deuteronomistic hand is responsible for the present form of chapter 12.[120] All of the scholars who fit into
the above categories are agreed that the outlook of chapter 12
is clearly anti-monarchical, perhaps even to a greater extent
than other materials in the so-called late source. Corresponding to this is a great emphasis on the importance of Samuel
who appears here as both mediator and intercessor. Only a few
scholars have differed with this majority opinion by challenging the essential unity of the chapter, but their analyses have
not been convincing. Seebass fragments the chapter in a manner
that owes more to the demands of historical reconstruction than
to literary or form critical considerations.[121] M. Buber
limits the original material in the chapter to vss. 1-5 and
24-25, mostly on the grounds that the material hostile to the
kingship could not have been original.[122]

A careful examination of chapter 12 shows that there is
some basis for challenging the essential unity of the chapter
as a whole. The main seam that appears is to be found in vs.
6 which seems to be a completely new beginning. In 12:1 Samuel
begins an address to all Israel, and as is customary in verbal
exchanges, the verb alone is used in vs. 5 without a repetition
of the subject to identify the speaker. However, in vs. 6 the
entire address formula is found again identifying Samuel as the
speaker and the people (העם) as the listeners. What follows in
the MT of vs. 6 is confused. As it stands we have only the
divine name, יהוה, followed by two relative clauses which fail
to make a complete sentence. Most scholars have accepted the
LXX reading as most likely and have inserted the word עד to
read "Yahweh is witness, who..." This reading has led some to
assert that vs. 6 then goes properly with vss. 1-5 where the
motif of witness is also prominent. A closer examination renders this view untenable. Yahweh has already been invoked as

witness in vs. 5, and it is completely unnecessary to repeat
this in vs. 6 especially with another full introduction to the
speech of Samuel. Further, the use of עד in both verses is
entirely different. In vs. 5 it is clear that Yahweh (and his
anointed) is called upon to witness to Samuel's blamelessness
in the conduct of his office. McCarthy[123] has stated that the
use of עד in vs. 6 should be seen as covenantal. He notes that
the invocation of divine witnesses often stood at the head of
treaty forms and that the relative clauses which follow "function less as history than as a solemn designation of Yahweh."
Thus, vs. 6 would form a suitable introduction to what follows
in vss. 7ff., the covenantal form of which we shall discuss below. It is possible that vss. 1-5 do not constitute an original part of vss. 6ff. but represent an independent tradition.
It may be that the common use of עד provided the occasion for
the juncture of the two traditions despite the different usage
made of the word. Such combination by means of catchword is
certainly not unknown in the Old Testament. Our judgment on
this will have to be reserved for a closer look at vss. 1-5 below.

Those who have defended the unity of chapter 12 have
pointed to vs. 13 as exhibiting dependence on vss. 1-2. Both
constitute a presentation of the king by Samuel which in itself
raises the question of why two such presentations would be
necessary. Both vs. 2 and vs. 13 begin with the forceful ex-
clamation ועתה הנה המלך, but the context of this usage in both
verses is completely different and only serves to emphasize the
independence of vss. 1-5 from vss. 6ff. In vs. 2 the king is
presented by Samuel to the people to demonstrate that he has
fulfilled their request in making them a king. The presentation of the king also serves as a motive for Samuel's seeming
retirement due to old age in vss. 3ff. Vs. 13 presents the
king in order to demonstrate the wilfullness of the people in
demanding a king. Here it is not Samuel who makes a king, but
the people have themselves chosen him, and Yahweh has simply
allowed it. The demand of the people for a king is an act of
rebellion which Yahweh has permitted.[124] This picture is in
contrast to that of vss. 1-5 where the king is described as

'Yahweh's anointed' (vss. 3, 5), a designation which does not appear in the rest of the chapter. Again this might indicate that vss. 1-5 were originally independent of 12:6ff.

Some have felt that vs. 25 shows knowledge of the fall of Jerusalem and is to be considered a post-exilic addition. The use here of the infinitive absolute + a finite verb following the conditional particle אם is particularly emphatic in comparison with the previous verses. It does not seem unlikely that the verse is a late addition, but the evidence is inconclusive.

Before any conclusions can be drawn on the development of the chapter into its present form, we must look more closely at the character and origins of the various materials in the chapter.

Vss. 1-5 form a well-organized unit centering on the proclamation of Samuel's innocence in the conduct of his office and it is usually understood to imply his resignation or retirement. This view is probably correct in light of Samuel's stress on his age and length of service in connection with his presentation of the king in vs. 2. The first three elements of the unit are given force by the use of the exclamatory particle הנה, which introduces Samuel's opening statement recalling the people's past request for a king (vs. 1). In vs. 2, the even more forceful expression ועתה הנה is used to introduce the climactic point of the unit. The king is now before them and Samuel is old; there is need for a change. From this assertion that a turning point has been reached, Samuel then introduces the matter of immediate concern with הנני. Vss. 3-4 seem to contain some sort of ceremony exonerating Samuel from all blame in the conduct of his office. G. von Rad has recognized that this section is related to the *Gattung* of the confessional list.[125] These lists usually consist of a series of negative statements protesting innocence of any transgressions in regard to certain commandments (e.g. Num. 16:15; Deut. 26:13-14). As von Rad has noted, the name "confessional list" is not very appropriate since the worshipper is claiming complete innocence rather than confessing sin. In I Sam. 12:3-4 we do not have the usual list form but a series of questions which surely have their roots in such a list:

אֵת שׁוֹר מִי לָקַחְתִּי
וַחֲמוֹר מִי לָקַחְתִּי
וְאֶת מִי עָשַׁקְתִּי
אֶת מִי רַצּוֹתִי
וּמִיַּד מִי לָקַחְתִּי כֹפֶר

Von Rad has noted that the question form coupled with the admonition to testify against Samuel (עֲנוּ בִי) seems to suggest a
legal rather than the usual cultic setting.[126] However, the
list of questions is followed by a congregational response, and
the people are called upon in vs. 3 to "testify against me *before Yahweh* and *before his anointed*." The concern here might
be best located in the realm of sacral law. Again in vs. 5
when Samuel's absolution is followed by formulae of witness,
which is clearly a legal term, the witnesses are to be Yahweh
and his anointed. We have already noticed a concern for
sacral/legal matters in the prophetically-influenced materials
in I Sam. 7-11. Certainly there seem to be ties between 12:1-5
and some of the prophetic material already examined. Vs. 1 is
clearly related to 8:7 and 22 where Samuel is commanded to
"hearken to the voice of the people." Further in 8:22 Samuel
is commanded to "make them a king," and in 12:1 he reports that
he has fulfilled this mission. Samuel does not appear as the
maker of the king in 12:6ff. The use of the title מָשִׁיחַ for the
king in 12:3 and 5 is also striking. Since the tradition that
Saul was anointed appears only in 9:16 and 10:1, it would appear that 12:3, 5 is dependent on that tradition. This certainly implies a rather positive attitude toward the king since
he is *Yahweh's* anointed. This is in contrast to the remainder
of chapter 12 which does not use this title for the king.
Another tie to earlier material might be seen in the fact that
the king as Yahweh's anointed plays a clear role in the testimony of vss. 3-4 and in the witnessing of vs. 5. We have
pointed out earlier that in 11:12-13 the concern seems to be to
show the transfer of certain sacral/legal responsibilities from
Samuel to the king. Thus, 12:1-5 would seem to form a logical
continuation of this concern, for it shows the king clearly
functioning in the sacral/legal realm and gives a picture of
Samuel seemingly retiring from office. All of these links to

earlier material are at points that have been previously designated as traditions that show the influence of a prophetic redactor and his concerns. I Sam. 12:1-5 is then to be seen as a
report added to the notice of an assembly at Gilgal in order to
record the ceremony of Samuel's public exoneration from blame.
It forms the end of the period of Samuel as the chief office
holder in Israel. It is the motif of witness, עד, in vs. 5
which attracted the supplementary material in vss. 6ff. since
it too deals with the witness motif although in a different
context. It is to an examination of this material (vss. 6ff.)
that we must now turn.

I Sam. 12:6-15 has long been recognized as an example of
the influence of the covenant form, although with variations
to be sure.[127] We have already seen that vs. 6 may well serve
as an introduction to the covenant form since the lists of divine witnesses often stood at the beginning of the treaties.[128]
Also in vs. 6 the maker of the covenant is identified in terms
of the relative clauses attached to the formula of divine witness. It should be noted that some of the variations in the
form are brought about by the simple fact that here we do not
have a covenant or treaty document but a speech by Samuel that
shows the influence of the covenant form. Samuel's role is
that of covenant mediator in the manner of Moses and Joshua.
The historical prologue here is a recitation of Yahweh's saving
acts with an emphasis on the people's rebellious nature (vss.
7-12), and this recitation is introduced in a manner similar to
Jos. 24:1 through the use of the verb יצב. This section is
also marked by the particle ועתה as is the transition to the
stipulations in vs. 13 and to the theophany in vs. 16. The
historical recitation starts with the delivery from Egypt,
briefly mentions the giving of the land and details the period
of the judges. Vs. 12 then brings the historical retrospect
up to the present with the introduction of the people's request
for a king. The transition from historical prologue to stipulations is marked by ועתה, as in Ex. 19:5 and Jos. 24:14, although I Sam. 12:13 adds additional climactic force through the
use of the exclamatory particle הנה. Vs. 13 represents a turning from past to present and is quite in keeping with the

covenantal form. It constitutes a presentation of the king,
and as McCarthy has noted, the treaties often show the vassal
invested with his throne in the stipulation section.[129]   He
also notes, however, that the parallel is an ambiguous one because of the unusual tone of the historical prologue. In the
treaties, the history provides a basis for the acceptance of a
king invested with his throne, but here the prologue implies
that the accession of a king represents some sort of infidel-
ity. This emphasis is carried on in the blessing/curse formula
in vss. 14-15. Whereas the usual formulation would be to in-
sure the proper functioning of the office of the king, the emphasis here is on the fidelity of the people. Further, the
apodosis of the blessing in vs. 14 is missing, and some have
felt this to be a further indication of the negative emphasis
of the passage. This is not a totally persuasive interpretation since the suppression of entire clauses which must be supplied from context (aposiopesis) seems to be common in conditional constructions (see GK 167a).[130]   In any case, it is
clear that I Sam. 12:6-15 shows the influence of the covenant
form (cf. Ex. 19:3-6 and Jos. 24), but it is equally clear that
it has here been varied to serve a particular purpose. Some
have suggested that the purpose is to condemn the kingship as
apostasy, but this is too strong. McCarthy has characterized
the function of the passage as a warning,[131] and this seems
more nearly accurate. The kingship is not condemned outright
even though its roots lie in the rebellious nature of the people. In vs. 13b, it is Yahweh who finally permits the people a
king, and it is quite clear that if the people follow Yahweh's
commandments it will go well with them *and* the king (vs. 14).
Kingship is not evil *per se*, but only as an instance of Israel's lack of faith. The emphasis throughout is on the people
and not the king, and it is to the purpose of confronting the
people with their sin that the covenant form is used here.
This is clearly indicated as early as vs. 7 when Samuel announces that his purpose is to "judge you before Yahweh"
(ואשפטה אתכם לפני יהוה). This is also clearly seen in vs. 19
when following the covenantal recitation of Samuel and the theophanic sign of vss. 16-18 the people confess their sin and
call to Samuel for intercession.

In vss. 16-18, Samuel's covenantal speech is followed by the giving of a sign. These verses are introduced in a manner similar to vs. 7 with the phrase גם-עתה התיצבו. The giving of a sign to confirm the authority of a previous message is not uncommon (Isa. 7:10-16). Here the miracle of rain in the dry season carries overtones of theophany. Samuel does not perform the sign but calls upon Yahweh to send thunder and rain. Thunder (קול) is a common theophanic manifestation. Ex. 19:19 shows a theophany involving thunder which follows a covenantal formulation. The response of the people also seems to be more appropriate to a theophany than to a mere sign. In the request for Samuel to intercede for them in 12:19, the people express the fear, as they did in Deut. 5:25 (connected with קול), that they will die. The formula of reassurance, אל-תיראו, in vs. 20, appears elsewhere as a response to theophany in Jdgs. 6:23 where it is connected with the fear of death. Seebass has argued that the theophany and the people's response in 12:16-25 are parallel to and dependent on 7:5-12.[132] It is true that we have a theophany in both passages but the context is entirely different; that of 7:5-12 is holy war while that of 12:16-25 is covenantal.[133]

Before considering the remaining section of the chapter we must take a closer look at the language and themes used in 12:7ff. to see if they will give us any clue to the identity of the hand responsible for this section built around the covenantal form. Is the section Deuteronomistic in character? Certainly there are links to earlier material in I Sam. 7-11 that has been identified as Deuteronomistic. The theme of apostasy from Yahweh and the service of foreign gods appeared earlier in 7:3-4 and 8:8 and is now to be found in 12:10. Here, as in 7:4, the foreign gods are specifically identified as Baals and Ashtaroth (בעלים, עשתרות). Accompanying the apostasy theme, the positive admonition to serve (עבד) Yahweh is found in 7:3 and 12:14. The verb עזב, often favored by the Deuteronomistic writer for describing Israel's apostasy, was seen in 8:8 and appears again in 12:10. Broadening the scope of our comparison, it is also possible to say that 12:7ff. bears a striking resemblance to materials generally agreed upon as Deuteronomistic in the Book of Judges (Jdgs. 2:11ff.; 3:7ff.; 10:6ff.). There again the service of foreign gods and Israel's apostasy are major themes. The cycle of apostasy, punishment, cry for help, and delivery described in Jdgs. 2: 11ff. is also found in I Sam. 12:9-11. A brief chart will best show the striking similarity in the use of verbs among various Deuteronomistic passages:

	Jdgs.			I Sam.		Jos.
עבד	3:7	2:11	10:6		12:10	
עזב		2:12	10:6	8:8	12:10	24:16, 20
שכח	3:7				12:9	
מכר	3:8	2:14	10:7		12:9	
זעק + confession of sin			10:10		12:10	

It would seem clear that we have in I Sam. 12:7ff. another of the Deuteronomistic historian's programmatic passages similar to those found in the Book of Judges, though here couched in the form of a direct address by Samuel. It serves to show the period of the kingship as originating solely in the grace of Yahweh and in spite of the people's rebellious will. The people sinned in asking for a king, but Yahweh responds once again in grace.

A brief word should be said about vs. 12 which mentions the incident with Nahash the Ammonite. This verse is important in helping us to relate chapter 12 to the materials which now precede it. It would seem that the writer knew the tradition of chapter 11, but the quotation of the people's demand for a king in 12:12b also shows that he knew of the tradition preserved in 8:19. It is clear, however, that the whole of chapters 8 and 12 does not stem from the same hand since this request is now placed in an entirely different context in 12:12. It would seem likely that the Deuteronomistic editor found the combined materials recording the rise of Saul in an edition that had the Ammonite War as the last major incident confirming Saul's kingship. This was then clearly the culminating event in the outcome of the people's request for a king. In any case the verse clearly shows the original independence of 12:7ff.

from any of the major Saul traditions in chapters 7-11, although there is a relationship between chapter 12 and the Deuteronomistic portions of chapter 8.

After the theophany of 12:16-18 and the confessional response of the people in vs. 19, Samuel again addresses the people in terms of themes familiar from the earlier covenantal formulation. Vss. 20-25 repeat the stipulation urging service to Yahweh and turning from apostasy (vss. 20-21) and repeat the blessing and cursing (vss. 22, 24-25). Vs. 24 is a curious insertion which pictures Samuel both as intercessor and teacher. McCarthy has noted that Deut. 29-30 and Jos. 23 show a similar pattern of a complete covenant form, an interruption (here the sign of vss. 16-18 and the confession of vs. 19), and a return to covenant themes in a less formal style.[134] Certainly vss. 20-25 lack the more formal structure of vss. 7-15. Its character is that of preaching or admonition, and the role of Samuel has changed accordingly in vs. 23. He is no longer the covenant mediator of vss. 7ff. The style is that of parenesis known best from the framework of Deuteronomy, and there too we find the covenant mediator, Moses, in the role of preacher and teacher. The general theme of 20-25 is again one familiar in Deuteronomic and Deuteronomistic material. The people are urged to serve Yahweh "with all your heart" (cf. Deut. 4:29; 6:5; 10:12; 11:13; Jos. 23:14; I Sam. 7:3; 12:20, 24) and to turn aside from false gods. There would seem little reason not to conclude that in vss. 20-25 the same Deuteronomistic writer responsible for vss. 6-19 has simply finished the unit with a brief final exhortation by Samuel. Thus, the structure of the Deuteronomistic section of the chapter would look as follows:

> 6-15 Covenantal formulation - addressed to the people
> for the purpose of confronting them with their
> faithlessness.
>
> 16-18 Theophanic sign - adds force and authority to the
> above.
>
> 19   Request for intercession and confession of sin - by
> people.
>
> 20-25 Closing admonition - addressed to people by Samuel.

If I Sam. 12:6-25 is from a Deuteronomistic hand, what can be concluded concerning the attitude toward the kingship displayed here? Most scholars have felt it to be decidedly negative. This, however, is hard to reconcile with the redemptive tone of the chapter. To be sure, the people have sinned in asking for a king, but this is set in the context of Israel's tendency to turn to foreign gods in the period of the judges, and the asking of a king is sinful only because it represents a turning from Yahweh. The people confess this sin, and their election as God's people is reaffirmed (vs. 22). Further, it is clear that God is to allow Israel a king, and if Israel and her king are obedient to God's will, they will both be blessed (vss. 13-15). This could hardly be characterized as unalterably opposed to the monarchy. In fact, the monarchy as such is secondary to the major theme of the people's sinful will and God's constant redemption. If God's word is obeyed even the kingship can work to his will, it is only when the kingship acts as an instrument of rebellion that it is evil. Indeed, with the promise to David in II Sam. 7 (usually taken as showing Deuteronomistic influence) the attitude toward the kingship is clearly positive. I Sam. 12 and II Sam. 7 may be related in the concept of the divine name as an agent of reconciliation. In 12:22, Israel's election is reaffirmed "for his great name's sake." In II Sam. 7:26, the Davidic dynasty becomes the bearer of the glory of God's name. The kingship is born in Israel's willful nature but is transformed by Yahweh into the agency of his reconciliation with Israel. McCarthy has reflected on the relationship of I Sam. 12 and II Sam. 7 as follows:[135]

> The overriding theological principle is that Yahweh's word is infallible. Even though it be frustrated in a given instance it will eventually be fulfilled. The same principle is at work in Deut. 1, where the desert generation sins and is denied the promised land (vs. 35) but the succeeding generation is assured possession of the land (vs. 39) because the promise to the patriarchs is still valid as is apparent even in vs. 35. One might even ask if the disappearance of Saul and his family, the concrete embodiment of Israel's sinful self-will, is not thought of as a parallel with the death of the desert generation leaving the way open for the guiltless successor.

* * *

We may summarize our results as follows:

A.   The section in 12:1-5 is not of a piece with vss. 6-25 but does show links with earlier material.   It is concerned with the ritual establishment of Samuel's innocence in the conduct of his office and seems to indicate his retirement from at least a portion of his duties because of age and the presence of a king in Israel.   The unit shows clear evidence of connections with chapters 8, 10 and 11, and as in 11:12-13 it shows the king taking up responsibilities in sacral/legal matters which probably belonged to the office of Samuel previously.

B.   The Deuteronomistic editor, perhaps prompted by the motif of witnessing in vs. 5, has taken the occasion of Samuel's speech to formulate one of the programmatic speeches which mark the turning points of the Deuteronomistic history work.   The main section of the speech is built around the covenantal form (vss. 6-15), and this is followed by a theophanic sign (vss. 16-18), a confession (vs. 19), and a closing exhortation (vss. 20-24).   Vs. 25 may belong with the final exhortation or it may be a post-exilic addition; the evidence is unclear.   The theme of this speech is the sinful self-will of the people which has now manifested itself in the desire for a king.   The kingship as such is not condemned in absolute terms, and the implication is clearly present that through obedience to God's will the king as well as the people can enjoy the blessing of God.   This entire section (vss. 6-25) was added after the previous material in chapters 7-11 had been brought together by a previous editorial hand, and this later redactor apparently meant his work at this point to be supplementary to that of the earlier edition.

I Samuel 13

The great majority of scholars who have worked on the critical problems of First Samuel have agreed that the material in chapter 13 concerning Saul's military encounters with the Philistines belongs with the so-called early source while the rejection episode in vss. 7b-15a is to be regarded as a secondary addition to the chapter at a later time under the influence of the account in chapter 15.[136]   These scholars are in general agreement on the character of vss. 2-7a, 15b-22 as old, archival material with some evidence of popular embellishment in certain details. These verses are generally regarded as close to the events they describe and as fruitful material for use in historical reconstruction. However, these same scholars show a wide diversity in their interpretations of vss. 7b-15a. After agreeing that these verses came secondarily into the text scholars are at odds on the nature of the incident described in vss. 7b-15a, its function in its present context and its relationship to the similar account in chapter 15. There are those whose view of chapter 13 does not conform to the prevailing opinion.[137] Most of these scholars attempt some type of source division within the chapter, and their results are neither uniform nor convincing. A few have found Deuteronomistic influence in the chapter. For example, Schunck[138] labels the whole of vss. 7b-15a as Deuteronomistic, while Seebass[139] sees Deuteronomistic influence only in 13:1,[140] 13bα, 14bβγ. However, Noth himself would disagree. He, of course, attributes the chronological note in 13:1 to the Deuteronomist, but he then states: "Im übrigen haben wir keine einzige sichere Spur einer Bearbeitung der Sauls-Geschichte I Sam. 13,1--2 Sam. 2,7 durch Dtr."[141] He goes on to state that he would regard vss. 7b-15a as secondary, but he sees no hint there of Deuteronomistic influence. Noth's view on chapter 13 can thus be classed with the general concensus.

The major literary critical observation to be made in chapter 13 has already been mentioned in our brief survey of scholarly opinion on the chapter. The section in vss. 7b-15a on the conflict between Samuel and Saul is not of a piece with the remainder of the chapter but must have been inserted secondarily. This is most clearly seen in an examination of the difficulties connected with Saul's apparent change of location from Gibeah to Gilgal and back to Gibeah again. When the narrative opens, Saul and Jonathan are both in the area around Gibeah of Benjamin (vss. 2-3), and following Jonathan's skirmish with the Philistines, Saul apparently moves to Gilgal where the people are called out to join him (vs. 4). In response to Jonathan's victory, the Philistines move troops into

Michmash and make camp there separated only by a deep valley
from Gibeah (vs. 5). Vs. 7b makes quite clear that as the text
stands Saul is still in Gilgal, and vs. 8 relates that he remained there seven days waiting for the arrival of Samuel. Vs.
16, however, presents a major difficulty when it states that
Saul and his men had been camped at Gibeah of Benjamin[142] when
the Philistines had encamped opposite them at Michmash. Syntactically, there is no other way to read the verse. The first
half of the verse uses a participial construction (ישבים) to
indicate continuous action. This clearly contrasted with the
second half of the verse which is a circumstantial clause (indicated by the placement of the subject before the verb) with a
perfect verb (חנו).[143] In light of this contrast, one must
read the verse to indicate that at the time the Philistines
camped at Michmash, Saul and Jonathan continued to be camped at
Gibeah.[144] This would make any movement of Saul to Gilgal impossible and thus stands in sharp contrast to the earlier portion of the chapter. It would appear that originally the account of Saul's military encounters with the Philistines included no trip to Gilgal. The only reference to Gilgal outside
of the block of material in vss. 7b-15a is at the end of vs. 4,
and this could easily have been a harmonizing addition. Several minor observations lend support to the contention that vs.
16 shows the episode in Gilgal to be a secondary addition to
the narrative. In vss. 5-6, the Philistines move an army to
Michmash, and the Israelite troops either skirmish with them or
are frightened off without a fight. In either case, this could
not, as the chapter now stands, be an encounter with Saul's
main force since he is apparently in Gilgal (vs. 7b). However,
in vs. 15 Saul returns to Gibeah (reading with LXX) but he has
only six hundred men. The trip to Gilgal for a general call to
arms has been singularly unfruitful. Saul started with two
thousand men, made a general call to arms, did not engage the
enemy and is left with only six hundred men. Again it is the
muster at Gilgal which has confused the picture. As a further
minor argument in this matter, it must be noted that in the
continuation of this narrative of Saul's Philistine encounters
in chapter 14,[145] the rejection in 13:7b-15a has no effect and

receives no mention. The prevailing opinion among scholars
that 13:7b-15a is a later insertion into the chapter seems
well-founded. We must now turn for a closer look at the character of the materials in the chapter.

In 13:1 we find the formula customarily used to introduce
the reign of a king in the Book of Kings (e.g. I Kgs. 14:21;
22:42). It states the king's age at accession and the number
of years he occupied the throne. The same formula is used for
Ishbaal (II Sam. 2:10) and David (II Sam. 5:4). Since all of
the material on Saul prior to chapter 13 deals with his becoming king, 13:1 is clearly the obvious place for the use of the
formula to introduce his reign. Here, however, the formula
seems incomplete. The Masoretic text reads literally that
Saul was one year old when he began to reign. Comparison with
other occurrences of the formula makes clear that a number has
either dropped out or been purposely omitted between בן and
שנה. Three manuscripts of the LXX give Saul an age of thirty
years, but this seems a little low in view of the necessary age
of Jonathan a few verses later. The editor may have simply
lacked information on Saul's age and left it blank. A further
difficulty in this verse lies in the figures for the length of
Saul's reign. The text as it stands tells us that Saul ruled
for two years (ושתי שנים), but this numerical form is found no-
where else in Biblical Hebrew. The proper form for two years
is שנתים (e.g. I Kgs. 15:25). The form שנים שתים appears in
II Sam. 2:10 and II Kgs. 21:19 (II Chron. 33:21). In addition
to this grammatical problem, scholars have often suggested that
two years is too short for Saul's reign and emended to read
either twelve or twenty-two years although there is no textual
support for this reading.[146] Josephus (Ant. 6.14.9) and Acts
13:21 both read forty years which is a round figure often used
in the historical books (e.g. for David in II Sam. 5:4). These
difficulties and the absence of the verse from a large number
of LXX manuscripts caused many earlier commentators to view
13:1 as a later attempt to give Saul a formula on the analogy
of those for David and the later kings.[147] However, Martin
Noth, in his hypothesis of a Deuteronomistic history work, has
argued that such formulae are characteristic of the Deuteronomistic editor, and it would be much more unusual for the text

not to contain a formula for Saul.[148] Noth would also defend
the two-year figure for Saul's reign. He feels the Deuteronomist intended to write two years since this fits his chronological scheme. He believes the ושתי שנים form to be unusual but
grammatically possible. Further, Noth would claim the two-year
figure to have a sound historical basis since Saul's reign was
a short-lived phenomenon and the Deuteronomist could have built
his chronological scheme up at other points rather than invent
a figure for this important period.[149] In any case, there is
little reason to dispute Noth's contention that 13:1 is the introductory formula to Saul's reign placed there by the Deuteronomist as a part of his total chronological system. Saul's
age seems to have been left out due to lack of information or
confusion in the sources on this matter. The figure for the
length of Saul's reign is probably to be accepted inasmuch as
there are no textual variants at this point and two years seems
to fit the Deuteronomistic chronology.

The material in 13:2-7a, 15b-23 all deals in some way with
the hostilities between the Philistines and Israel under Saul.
Some scholars have felt the narrative to be rather confused,
but the removal of the Gilgal episode in vss. 7b-15a and the
reference to Gilgal in vs. 4b leave a rather straightforward
account. Saul is at Michmash and Jonathan at Gibeah (vs. 2);
the attack by Jonathan on the Philistine garrison at Gibeah
(vs. 3a) gains wide notice (vss. 3b-4a), and it is known that
the Philistines have become aroused. Saul then calls out the
levy in vs. 4b. The Philistines send a large force which camps
at Michmash, and this is apparently followed by a general panic
among the men of Israel (vss. 5-7a). In vs. 15b, Saul is left
with only six hundred men in Gibeah facing the Philistines who
are still encamped at Michmash. This establishes the setting
for the events which follow in chapter 14. There would seem to
be nothing awkward or confusing in this course of events.

There is little that need be said concerning the material
in 13:2-7a, 15b-18, 23.[150] Its concern is almost solely with
the numbers and movements of troops for both Israel and the
Philistines. The general style of this material is terse and
reportorial. There is no use of dialogue and little concern

for the personalities involved, but it is filled with details
of numbers and places (e.g. the numbers and locations of Saul's
troops in vs. 2, the numbers, types and deployment of the Philistines in vs. 5, and the deployment and routes of the Philistine patrols in vss. 17-18). The material is almost bare of
stylistic devices but unfolds in a straightforward manner. Only in vss. 5-6 do we find the more literary phrase "like the
sand on the seashore in number" followed by a temporal clause
and a כי clause that states the situation which results in the
action of the next main verb. This same construction is used
in the report of the Ammonite war narrative in II Sam. 10:6, 9,
15. The conclusion can hardly be avoided that we are dealing
with material drawn from official records of some sort. The
abundance of concrete detail, the lack of dialogue and character development, and the compact style all mark this material
as probably annalistic in origin.

The function of the military material in chapter 13 seems
to be to set the scene for the account in chapter 14. It is
fairly clear that the two chapters are closely related. Most
of these relationships have been noted before so we need not
dwell at length on them. Jonathan's deed in 13:2 may be intended to foreshadow his daring in chapter 14. The general panic
of the Israelites in 13:6-7a describes them as hiding in caves
and serves as the background to the Philistines' comment in
14:11. The reference to Saul's number of troops as six hundred
is repeated in 14:2. Finally, 13:23 seems to be a note on
Philistine troop movements which serves as a transition to the
action about to begin in chapter 14. The word used here for
garrison (מצב) appears in 14:1, 4, 6, 11, 12, and the word
מעבר, "pass," seems to represent the same location referred to
in 14:4 by מעברות.

The military material in chapter 13 also seems to show a
connection to chapter 10. In 13:3, Jonathan precipitates hostilities by defeating the garrison (נציב)[151] of the Philistines
at Gibeah.[152] The same garrison (נציב) is mentioned in 10:5.
Scholars have unanimously felt this to show a link between the
two sections, but it is difficult to determine the nature of
the connection. We would note that 10:5 is in a section

earlier ascribed to a redactor's hand, and we would suggest
that the connection shows that the redactor in 10:5 knew of
the tradition in 13:2ff. However, we will reserve further comment on the relationship of chapters 10 and 13 until we have
examined 13:7b-15a and its connection to 10:8.

Only a brief comment is necessary on the note in vss. 19-
22. This note does not concern military movements at all but
records the fact that the Philistines had a monopoly on metalworking. The Israelites even had to have common implements
sharpened by the Philistines, and only Saul and Jonathan had
swords. This brief section is an obvious diversion from the
course of the main narrative, but the inclusion of such details
as the charge for sharpening implements suggests that it should
be regarded as genuinely old tradition. There is no way of
determining when this note was inserted into the narrative, but
it is of little importance. It might be conjectured that one
of the purposes for this brief aside was to heighten the dramatic quality of the victory in chapter 14.

We have already seen that vss. 7b-15a must be regarded as
a secondary addition to the chapter. In this case it is apparent that vss. 7b and 15b serve as the connecting links. In vs.
7b the location of the following event is established as Gilgal, and in vs. 15a (LXX)[153] Saul is returned from Gilgal to
Gibeah of Benjamin for the continuation of the narrative on
Saul's military activities against the Philistines.

The remaining material (vss. 8-14) constitutes a definite
literary type which may be profitably examined. In form, this
section might be identified in a preliminary manner as a prophetic oracle of judgment pronounced against an individual.[154]
As we shall see, our passage represents something of a variant
of this formal type since it is completely embedded in a narrative context (as is 15:16ff. and II Sam. 12). Its elements,
however, are still clearly distinguishable:

Introduction, vss. 8-10 - This element is not a firmly
established part of the prophetic speech form but is formulated
according to the context in which the judgment oracle is found.
When the speech is completely embedded within a narrative setting, the introduction tends to be more elaborate, setting the

scene and describing the circumstances which lead up to the
confrontation between the prophet and the individual against
whom the oracle is directed. This is certainly the case in 13:
8-10 as well as in I Sam. 15 and II Sam. 12. In our passage,
Saul has fulfilled the requirement of Samuel that he wait seven
days,[155] but Samuel has not arrived and his troops are scatter-
ing. He thus proceeds with the sacrifices,[156] whereupon Samuel
arrives just as he has finished. In light of the situation, it
is hard to consider these sacrifices as other than those which
precede the battle in the holy war,[157] and we have already seen
a tradition ascribing this function to Samuel in 7:9-10. When
Saul goes out to meet Samuel in vs. 10, we have been given all
the elements necessary for understanding the conflict which en-
sues.

   Accusation, vss. 11-13a - The accusation can take the form
of either an assertion (II Sam. 12:9b; I Kgs. 14:9; Amos 7:16)
or an accusing question (I Sam. 2:29; II Sam. 12:9a; I Kgs.
21:18; II Kgs. 1:3; Isa. 7:13; 22:16). In I Sam. 13:11, the
accusing question can be distinguished, but the exact nature of
the transgression is not stated in it (מה עשית). The same is
true in I Sam. 15:14 and II Kgs. 20:14f. However, the purpose
of the accusing question is to establish the facts involved
which are to call forth judgment, and this is adequately done
by Saul's answer to the accusing question in vss. 11b-12.
Saul's answer is similar to testimony given in a hearing.
Westermann has recognized the judicial nature of the accusing
question: "The prophetic accusation to an individual person was
often a matter of the prophet's establishing the facts of the
case through questions exactly as it occurs in the regular
judicial process... (It is) similar to a hearing in which the
prophet is one who hears and the king is the one heard."[158] It
is an interesting dramatic touch that in Saul's answer to Samuel the narrator has him attempt to shift the blame for the incident to Samuel as shown by the emphatic use of the independent pronoun, אתה, in vs. 11. Interestingly, the accusation
also appears in its declaratory form in vs. 13a (נסכלת לא שמרת
את-מצות יהוה אלהיך אשר צוך). Again the exact nature of the
grounds for the accusation is left unclear, but the preceding

account makes clear that the narrator regards Saul as guilty of
exceeding his own authority by infringing on the responsibilities delegated to Samuel, thus exceeding his own authority.
Since our knowledge of office and authority in this period is
limited, the transgression does not appear as sharply defined
as we could wish. The declaratory accusation in vss. 13a
simply makes clear that Saul's action is interpreted as a violation of God's law. It then becomes Samuel's duty as God's
prophetic messenger to proclaim God's judgment on Saul for this
violation.[159]

Announcement, vss. 13b-14 - Usually the announcement is
introduced by a variation of the messenger formula or at least
by הנה. It is possible that the use of the emphatic temporal
particle, ועתה, in vss. 13b and 14 is intended as a brief introduction, but it is not uncommon for it to be missing when
the prophetic speech is placed entirely within a narrative context (I Sam. 15:16ff.; II Sam. 12). In form, the announcement
consists of a simple statement of the punishment which is to
befall the accused. In the earlier form, as here, this is
given in the third person in a face-to-face encounter. Only
later does the first person form of a speech by God himself appear. The simple announcement of judgment is found here in vs.
14a. Often in the judgments against individuals the announcement of judgment is contrasted with blessings that Yahweh has
given the accused or promises that might have been established
(I Sam. 2:30; 15:17-19; II Sam. 12:7b-9; I Kgs. 14:7f.), and
this contrast motif appears in our text in vs. 13b. Westermann
characterizes the type of judgment shown here as that which announces dispossession of the kingdom and links it with I Sam.
15:28 and I Kgs. 11:31.[160] A careful reading, however, shows
that Saul is not here being removed from the kingship, but he
is being cut off from the possibility of dynasty. In vs. 13b
the potential that Saul might have enjoyed was that "the Lord
would have established your kingdom over Israel forever," הכין
יהוה את-ממלכתך אל-ישראל עד-עולם. This is clearly reminiscent
of the promises given to David establishing his dynasty in II.
Sam. 7:12, 16 (והכינתי את-ממלכתו, 12b; כסאך יחיה נכון עד-עולם,
16b). The judgment in vs. 14 states that Saul's kingdom "shall

not continue," ממלכתך לא-תקום, and the "man after his own
heart" whom Yahweh has made, נגיד, is here not Saul's replace-
ment, but his successor. Subsequent developments make clear
that this successor is David. In I Sam. 25:30 and II Sam. 6:21
he is referred to as נגיד. Thus, the thrust here must be described as the denial of dynasty, and its closest parallel is
perhaps the judgment against the house of Eli in I Sam. 2:31.
One further matter should be noted in the form of the announcement here. In vs. 14b, there is a reiteration of the accusation linked causally to the announcement (כי לא שמרת את אשר-צוך
יהוה). This type of relationship between accusation and announcement has been shown by Westermann to be a later development from the original form of the oracle[161] and is also found
in 15:23.

Our formal analysis of 13:8-14 allows us to draw several conclusions concerning the setting in which this tradition was
preserved. Westermann has the following to say on the period
of the form: "The judgment-speech to individuals had its proper
time in the period of the kings *before* the writing prophets.
The prophetic judgment-speech (that is found only in a narrative context), which has come down to us from this time, is ex-
clusively a judgment-speech to the individual and almost always
to the king. A few examples extend into the time of the writing prophets only to disappear completely after that."[162] Our
particular example in 13:8-14 shows the development of a stated
causal connection between the accusation and the announcement
(vs. 14b) which is a late development in the form. Thus, it
might be tentatively assigned to the period in the development
of the form close to or slightly overlapping the beginning of
the period of the writing prophets. If this conclusion is accepted, it then becomes impossible for us to assign this tradition to the Deuteronomist as a few have done. It seems clear
that it comes from prophetic circles dating roughly to the late
eighth century. Certainly the role of Samuel here is that of
God's prophetic messenger who confronts the king with his violations of God's law and pronounces judgment for that violation. Many have felt the prominence of sacrificial questions
here to show Samuel as a priestly figure,[163] but sacrifice in

this period cannot be regarded solely as a priestly perogative. Saul builds an altar with impunity in 14:35; Samuel is the blesser of the sacrifice in 9:13; Elijah offers sacrifice on Mt. Carmel in I Kgs. 18:20ff. It is not simply that Saul offered sacrifice, but that he proceeded with those sacral observances which precede the entry into battle without the presence of Samuel. We submit that these sacral acts are related to the holy war and the circles in which this tradition was preserved regarded the presence of the prophet as necessary. We have already noted Bach's study showing that the prophets took over the preservation of the functions relating to the holy war in the period of the monarchy,[164] and it would appear that Samuel is seen here in the role of the prophet who upholds the traditions of the holy war. Indeed this is, as we shall see, also the case in chapter 15, and we have already seen Samuel in the performance of sacral duties connected with holy war in chapter 7. The role of Samuel in 13:8-14 is quite in keeping with the conception of the prophet in the period of the divided monarchy.

A word must be added concerning the relationship of this section to other materials. We have already seen that 13:8 is connected with the instructions of Samuel in 10:8. The military traditions in chapter 13 are also connected to the same section in chapter 10 (13:3; 10:5). This clearly shows that the editor responsible for 10:5-8 knew both traditions found in chapter 13, and it is possible that he was responsible for their combination. There are also many comparisons that might be drawn between chapter 13 and the rejection account in chapter 15. An examination of this relationship will have to be left until we have done a careful analysis of chapter 15.

* * *

We may summarize our findings on I Samuel 13 as follows:

A.   Old traditions of an annalistic character are to be found in 13:2-7a, 15b-18, 23. They concern the numbers and movements of troops in Saul's early military encounters with the Philistines. In vss. 19-22 is another tradition recording the Philistine monopoly on metalworking. It is impossible to tell at what point this was brought into the text, but it appears to be an old tradition.

B.   A later editorial hand has inserted the tradition of the rejection of Saul's dynasty in vss. 7b-15a. He has added the reference to Gilgal in vs. 4 to harmonize the account since vss. 7b-15a seem to be firmly rooted at Gilgal. The form of the section as a judgment-speech to an individual and Samuel's role as guardian of the holy war functions and as pronouncer of judgment for the violation of God's law make clear that the tradition of vss. 7b-15a stems from prophetic circles dating roughly to the last half of the eighth century. The concern in the tradition seems to be to show why Saul was not to be given the promise of dynasty, and it thus opens the possibility for the dynastic promise to David, to whom reference is clearly made in vs. 14.

C.   Finally, the Deuteronomistic writer has added the chronological notice in 13:1, typical of the formulae used elsewhere in the Deuteronomistic work for the beginning of a king's reign. There is no evidence of Deuteronomistic influence in the remainder of the chapter.

I Samuel 14

This account of Jonathan's surprise attack on a Philistine garrison and the subsequent events of that day has provided little ground for controversy among scholars who have dealt with the problems of the composition of the Books of Samuel. It is true that Wellhausen expressed some doubts concerning the genuineness of vss. 36-45,[165] but his view was refuted by Budde, Smith and others[166] and has not gained widespread acceptance. A few scholars have felt that vss. 31-35 should be considered as a secondary addition to the narrative. A. Lods[167] felt that the section diverted from the focus on Jonathan in the rest of the chapter, and that it seemed to be almost a parallel to the sin of Jonathan in vss. 25-30. K. Schunck, more recently, has suggested that vss. 31-35 have been added by the Deuteronomist.[168] Despite these few disclaimers, it is apparent that an unusual degree of unanimity exists

among scholars as to the unity of the chapter through vs. 46.[169]
Even Eissfeldt has attributed the entire chapter (through vs.
51) to his old narrative source, L.[170] These scholars are
agreed that 14:1-46 is an old Saul tradition which probably is
to be dated close to the time of the events which the chapter
narrates. This narrative is connected to the Philistine war
material contained in chapter 13, thus forming an old but small
collection of material on Saul's activities against the Philistines. This collection is most often seen as incorporated into
the pro-Saul early source. Recently, H. Seebass[171] has challenged this scholarly consensus by proposing the following division of the chapter into two accounts: A. 14:2f., 6-13a,
15b,aβ, 13b, 20-22, 23b-29, 31, 36a, 37-46; B. 14:1, 4f., 14,
15aα, 16-18, 23a, 32-35, 30, 36b, 47-52. However, such whole-
sale division and rearrangement receives little support from a
careful study of the text and must be regarded as extremely
subjective. Concerning the summaries in vss. 47-51, scholars
are agreed that they can be considered to be secondary additions to the narrative of vss. 1-46,[172] but advance various
theories on the nature and significance of these summaries.[173]
Scholars are divided on the question of whether vs. 52 belongs
with the narrative of vss. 1-46 or with the summaries of 47-51.

On an initial survey of chapter 14, there might seem to be
a case for seeing the chapter as the combination of two originally separate accounts: one dealing with the surprise attack
by Jonathan, the subsequent battle, and concluding with the sin
of the people and Saul's altar (vss. 1-23, 31-35); and the
other concerning the sin of Jonathan and his redemption by the
people after Saul's oath condemns him to death (vss. 24-30,
36-46). Certainly the incident of the people's sin in eating
flesh with the blood in vss. 31-35 seems strangely to interrupt
the story of Jonathan's sin, and whereas Jonathan is made to
face the gravest of consequences for his offense, relatively
little is made of the people's cultic violation. Even those
scholars who have defended the unity of the chapter have expressed uneasiness concerning this section.[174] Further, vs.
31 contains the usual concluding formula for the pursuit following a holy war encounter (ה‍--מן--ויכו‍ or ‍עד--מן--ויכו‍),

and this would seem to connect well with vs. 23 containing the
delivery formula and the start of the pursuit. The notice of
Saul's altar building in vs. 35 would then form a fitting conclusion. A closer examination of the chapter, however, renders
any such division untenable. The evidence in its favor is almost completely subjective. A close literary-critical examination supports the general conclusion that the chapter must be
considered a unity through vs. 46. The reference to Ahijah the
priest and the ephod in vs. 3 is obviously meant to prepare the
reader for the reference to the priest in vs. 36. Further, the
oath of Saul committing the people to a fast is clearly seen in
the narrative as it now stands as the reason for the rash behaviour of the people in vss. 31-35. This can be seen from the
use of the very similar phrases in vss. 28b and 31b (וייעף העם,
28b; ויעף העם מאד, 31b).[175] The account of the people's sin
need not be considered unrelated to what follows either. After
the inquiry to God receives no answer in vs. 37, Saul places
the people on the one hand and himself and Jonathan on the
other for the casting of lots to determine the guilty party.
It is conceivable that the fact that at this point the reader
does not know whether Jonathan or the people will be designated
for their sins is an intentional part of the drama of the narrative. This would explain the unusual division for the lot-
casting rather than the narrowing-down procedure known to us
from Jos. 7 and I Sam. 10. In any case, there is no clear evidence to support any challenge to the unity of the chapter
through vs. 46. It is strange that vss. 31-35 are the only materials in the chapter which do not deal with Jonathan, and it
is possible that these verses represent an independent tradition in the pre-literary stage. Still it must be emphasized
that this is mere speculation, and as a literary unit, vss. 1-
46 must be considered to be a single piece. We must now turn
to a closer look at the nature of this narrative.

In general formation and style, the narrative of vss. 1-46
is typical of a broad type which we can label as the battle report. As a formal type, the battle report is very flexible,
but certain general patterns can be distinguished. W. Richter[176] has listed the following general elements common to the
battle reports of the Old Testament:

1. A verb of movement (בא, הלך, יצא).
2. This can be either preceded or followed by a verb belonging to the technical vocabulary of war (נלחם, אסף, חנה, צעק).
3. The following verb gives information on the outcome of the battle and differs with the object involved (city, לכד; men, נגף, נכה). It can also add reference to flight and pursuit (נוס, רדף).
4. A concluding element summarizes the totality of the victory which is won (מן- -- ועד, or מן- -- הַ + place names, מגפה גדולה, מכה גדולה).

Additional elements from the technical vocabulary of holy war often appear as well. (We will discuss the holy war aspects of the chapter in greater detail below.) Although even a cursory reading of the chapter shows that there is concern here for more than just a battle report, the general features noted by Richter are present in the section of the chapter dealing with Saul's entry into the fray after Jonathan's surprise attack.

14:20 (1 and 2) ויצעק -- ויבואו עד-המלחמה

23 ויושע (delivery formula from vocabulary of holy war)

31 (3) ויכו -- (4) מן -- הַ

Although portions of the chapter clearly show elements of the general category of a battle report, this is not sufficient to describe the chapter as a whole. As it now stands, vss. 1-46 form an extremely effective and dramatic literary composition which establishes Jonathan as a heroic figure in his attack on the Philistine garrison only to build the ensuing crisis to the climactic point that Jonathan's very life hangs in the balance. In contrast to the annalistic style of the Philistine war material in chapter 13, the section in 14:1-46 represents a more developed literary narrative. Since scholars are in general agreement concerning this contrast in styles between chapter 14 and 13:2-7a, 15b-23, it will suffice merely to mention a few of the general points of contrast. One of these is the general interest in the persons involved in the events. Jonathan and Saul appear as individuals rather than as mere names in a report. One of the devices which aids this is the

ample use of dialogue. Much of the dramatic movement of the
narrative is achieved through the use of direct speech. For
example, Jonathan discovers his inadvertent sin when one of the
people relates Saul's oath to him directly. The military material in chapter 13 is completely lacking in the use of dialogue. The writer in chapter 14 shows his flair for literary
effect in the very manner by which he begins his narrative. He
immediately introduces the point of action with Jonathan's proposal in vs. 1 before moving to the less interesting matters of
the *dramatis personae* and necessary topographical information
in vss. 2-5. Then, in an almost identical verse (6), he resumes the action he introduced in vs. 1. Much more could be
said on the stylistic devices employed by the writer in this
chapter, but this takes us beyond the purpose here. It will
suffice to say that we can see little reason to challenge the
usual conclusion that chapter 14 represents one of the finest
pieces of Hebrew narrative prose in the Old Testament.[177]

Beyond matters of general style, vss. 1-46 show the clear
influence of the holy war schema and its theology which have
already been discussed in connection with I Sam. 7. The schema
itself cannot be clearly distinguished here because it has been
completely absorbed into the narrative context, but all of its
individual elements are present.[178] Indeed, the decisive influence of Yahweh in fighting for Israel pervades the entire
chapter.

14:6   In the very making of his proposal for an attack on
the Philistine garrison, Jonathan affirms that it is
Yahweh who must in reality win the victory. His
power bears no relationship to numbers of men (אֵין
ליהוה מעצור להושיע ברב או במעט).

10,12   The entry into the fray has been made dependent on a
sign from Yahweh that he has given the Philistines
into their hands. This formula (נתן יהוה את-ביד-)
is one of the most typical formulae of the holy war
schema (Jos. 6:2, 12; 8:1, 7; 10:8, 12, 19; Jdgs.
11:30, 32; 12:3)[179] although it is usually found in
the context of the oracular inquiry of Yahweh (as in
vss. 36-37).

14:15   The enemy is stricken with God's panic, חרדת אלהים
(Gen. 35:5; Ex. 23:27; Isa. 2:10, 19), and there is
an earthquake.

  18   Saul begins to consult the oracles but does not
finish (see vss. 36-37).

  20   The enemy is thrown into confusion, מהומה גדולה
(cf. Jdgs. 7:22). More often the verbal form, הום,
is used (I Sam. 7:10; Ex. 14:24; Jos. 10:10; II
Sam. 22:15). There is a parallel to the turning of
the enemies' arms against one another in Jdgs.
7:22.

  23   The victory is ascribed to Yahweh by use of the delivery formula, ויושע יהוה ביום ההוא את-ישראל (I
Sam. 4:3; 7:8).

  31   Here we find one of the common formulae used to
conclude the holy war schema with a reference to
the totality of the victory, ויכו ביום ההוא בפלשתים
ממכמש אילנה (I Sam. 15:5-7; Num. 21:30; Jdgs. 11:
33; Jos. 10:10).

36-37 In an effort to renew the pursuit at night, Saul
attempts an oracular inquiry which shows the formula discussed in connection with vss. 10, 12 in its
more customary context.

  45   Even in the attempt to ransom Jonathan's life, the
people ascribe the victory to divine aid.

There can be little doubt that the narrative in 14:1-46 has
been greatly influenced by the language and theology of holy
war although it is impossible to detect here the clear-cut holy
war schema which we found in chapter 7. It would seem clear
that 14:1-46 can now be described as a narrative composition on
Jonathan's victory and subsequent sacrilege in which the author
has been influenced both by the standard, although loose,
structure of the battle report and the language and theology of
the holy war schema. Both of these influences have been rather
thoroughly absorbed into the writer's own narrative composition.

    In our discussion of the Philistine war material in chap-
ter 13 (2-7a, 15b-23), we have already had occasion to note

the close relationship between that material and 14:1-46.
There is no reason to go back over the connections noted previously. However, the nature of the relationship between the
two chapters is not yet entirely clear. We have noticed that
14:1-46 is stylistically quite different from the annalistic
type material in chapter 13. The differences are great enough
to make it highly unlikely that we are dealing simply with a
composition by a single writer. It seems more likely that what
is represented in chapters 13-14 is a small collection of material dealing with the Philistine war. A large portion of
this is the lengthy and detailed narrative of chapter 14 while
the background to this narrative is composed of annalistic materials from sources now unknown to us. It is entirely possible that the writer responsible for 14:1-46 also collected
the material in chapter 13 as background to his narrative.
This would certainly explain the clear connections between the
material, but such conclusions are merely speculation. In any
case, 13:2-7a, 15b-23; 14:1-46 can be considered as having been
drawn from narrative and annalistic sources and combined into a
small collection on the Philistine wars early in Saul's reign.

Just a word might be added on the function of 14:1-46 in
the larger structure of the section of I Samuel dealing with
the establishment of Saul's kingship (chapters 7-15). It is
interesting to note that Saul's commission in 9:16 was to be
God's chosen agent to deliver Israel from the Philistines. Although this account of Saul's commissioning occupies a prominent place in the material as we now have it, the carrying out
of this commission is not directly narrated. The material in
13:2-4 and 14:1-46 represents the only accounts we have of successful operations against the Philistines during Saul's reign.
Although it is admittedly speculative, it is at least suggestive to consider the possibility that the collection of material in chapters 13-14 functions in its present context as the
partial fulfillment of the commission in 9:16, a task which is
then interrupted by the final rejection of Saul in chapter 15.
In this same connection, we must look also at the summary in
14:47-48, for it too is positive concerning Saul's military
exploits.

It is not difficult to recognize that vss. 47-51 represent
a departure from the narrative which precedes it. Vss. 47-48
are clearly a summary of Saul's military deeds during his
reign, and vss. 49-51 give us Saul's genealogy. In the summary
are listed three peoples who are known to us as Saul's opponents from other materials (Ammon, the Philistines and the
Amalekites), and it is not in itself surprising to find that
Saul engaged in operations against other neighboring peoples.
In formal structure, there are no clear parallels, but it has
often been noticed that the peoples listed are similar to those
mentioned as David's opponents in II Sam. 8 and 10. Gressmann[180] felt these verses to be an unhistorical ascription of
David's victories to Saul, but Hertzberg has properly noted
that this is too hasty a conclusion.[181] There is no similarity
in form or order, and II Sam. 8 and 10 include various Aramaean
campaigns not listed in 14:47-48. In the absence of any further evidence, vss. 47-48 must be considered to refer to Saul
rather than to represent a borrowing. If this is the case,
then we have here a rather positive assessment of Saul's kingship. He is pictured as Israel's champion against her enemies.
Some have tried to read the final phrase of vs. 47 as implying
his rejection by translating ובכל אשר-יפנה ירשיע, "and wherever
he turned he was condemned." This seems highly unlikely. Vs.
48 immediately speaks of Saul's valor, ויעש חיל, and in any
case, the actual rejection of Saul from the kingship has not
yet taken place. Some have tried to overcome the difficulty by
translating "and wherever he turned he put them to the worse,"
which requires a rendering of the root in a sense unusual to
Biblical Hebrew. It would seem best to make a slight emendation in accordance with the LXX reading of ἐσώζετο and read
ויושע.[182] The phrase would then translate "wherever he turned
he was delivered (i.e. victorious)." A similar usage of the
root is found in II Sam. 8:6 where Yahweh is said to have delivered David wherever he went. The divine victory may lie behind the use of the niphal in 14:47. Some scholars have felt
vs. 48 to be a secondary addition on the basis of chapter 15
since this mention of the Amalekites is separated from the list
in vs. 47. However, this would be a strange addition on the

basis of chapter 15 which deals almost entirely with the
Amalekite war as the occasion for Saul's utter rejection. Vs.
48 characterizes the Amalekite campaign with the phrase ויעש
חיל, "and he did valiantly." Further, the notice appears before the account of the Amalekite war. It is hard to imagine
a reason for a later addition of a notice phrased in this manner and in this location which is said to be based on the tradition of chapter 15. The Amalekite notice must be considered
a genuine part of the summary.

It must now be asked when such a summary came into the
text. Since the Amalekite notice here precedes the account of
the Amalekite campaign in chapter 15, the summary must have
been placed here prior to inclusion in a larger context which
included chapter 15. Vs. 47 makes clear that this is intended
as a summary of Saul's deeds as king, and it would seem most
logical that these verses were originally attached as the conclusion to the small collection of materials in chapters 13-14.
Admittedly there is no strong evidence for such a conclusion,
but it is difficult to see why these summaries were not moved
to a later point in the larger collection of materials from the
period of Saul's kingship if they were not already firmly attached in their present position.

Vs. 52 is an interesting historical note, probably indicating Saul's attempt to create a professional army, but it is
difficult to relate to the surrounding materials. It may be
the conclusion of the collection in chapters 13-14, as indicated by the mention of the Philistine wars, or it may be a
transition note added later to make clear that despite Saul's
victory in chapter 14 the Philistines remained a threat. Those
who take the verse in the latter sense often see the reference
in the second half of the verse as a preparation for the account of David's attachment to the court of Saul in 16:14ff.
We can find no strong evidence for any conclusion on this verse.

* * *

To summarize our findings on I Sam. 14:
A. The narrative concerning Jonathan's surprise attack
and inadvertent sin in vss. 1-46 is probably based on old tradition. In its present form, it appears as a polished

literary piece which shows the clear influence of the general
structure of the battle report and of the vocabulary and theology of the holy war schema. The narrative is clearly connected
to material in chapter 13, and it is possible to regard these
two chapters, except for 13:7b-15a, as a small collection of
materials on Saul's military operations as king.

B.   The summary and genealogy in vss. 47-51 show a positive picture of Saul as the valiant military leader of Israel
in a troublesome time. The reference to Amalek in vs. 48 makes
it difficult to see the summary as having been inserted by a
late editorial hand. Its present position would indicate that
it was firmly attached to chapter 14 prior to the larger edition of materials on Saul's kingship. Hence, we view these
verses as the conclusion to the small collection of materials
on Saul's military operations in chapters 13-14. It is impossible to reach any conclusion on the relationship of vs. 52 to
the surrounding materials.

I Samuel 15

There has been a wider diversity in treating the relationship of chapter 15 to other materials than for any other chapter in the section of I Sam. 7-15. Most of the early scholars
placed chapter 15 in the so-called late source with chapters 7,
8, 10:17ff. and 12.[183] The usual argument was that the late
source was clearly anti-monarchical and the rejection of Saul
in chapter 15 was the logical climax for such a negative view
of the kingship. It was inevitable that the kingship would
lead to sin. We shall see the difficulties with such a view at
a later point. Related to those who placed chapter 15 in the
late source are a few scholars who have seen the chapter as
Deuteronomistically formulated.[184] However, they have usually
stressed that the Deuteronomist is drawing upon older material.
Seebass[185] is one of the few who have not felt the chapter to
be a unity. He sees two original accounts (A. 14:32-35; 15:1,
11, 12a, 16-19, 24-28; B. 15:2a, 3-9, 12b, 13f., 20b, 23, 29,
30a, 31a, 32-35a) which have been combined by a Deuteronomistic
editor whose traces are left in 15:2b, 6a, 10, 19a, bβ. Interestingly, Noth, who established the hypothesis of a Deuteronomistic history work, finds no clear indication of the

Deuteronomist's work in this chapter, although he does argue
that vss. 24-31 should be considered as secondary to the rest
of the chapter.[186] On the opposite side are those who would
relate chapter 15 to materials usually listed in the early
source. Mildenberger includes chapter 15 as part of a *nabi*-
istic redaction which includes 9:1-10:16 and 13:4b, 5, 7b-15a
on the basis of a connection to anointing.[187] Hertzberg feels
that chapter 15 was originally connected with chapter 11 and
that a later editor has broken this connection by inserting
chapters 12-14.[188] There are also scholars who would relate chapter 15 to materials in either the early or the late
source. Driver sees the chapter as intermediate between the
two source strands and belonging to neither.[189] Weiser views
it as an old, independent tradition which was later incorporated into a loose collection of materials showing prophetic influence.[190] It is obvious from this brief survey that there
are wide differences of opinion among scholars in regard to the
interpretation of I Samuel 15. It is with this in mind that we
turn ourselves to a closer examination of the chapter.

For the most part, scholars have defended the unity of
chapter 15. We have already seen that Seebass has, in a recent
article, attempted a radical division of the chapter, but this
seems to have been done on the basis of historical considerations rather than literary-critical evidence.[191] Pfeiffer and
Noth have both suggested that vss. 24-31 are secondary additions to the rest of the chapter,[192] but their evidence for
this remains obscure. Pfeiffer feels that these verses show
the religious moralizing tendency and the writing style of the
Deuteronomist who has thus reshaped older tradition material in
this chapter. He never explains this statement more fully.
Noth gives no evidence at all for his conclusion that vss. 24-
31 were added secondarily but merely states that these verses
show no evidence of a Deuteronomistic hand. With only these
brief allusions to guide us, it is difficult to see what made
these verses suspect. The section deals with Saul's attempt to
soften the judgment pronounced by Samuel by confessing his sin
of disobedience, and with the symbolic tearing of Samuel's robe
and the oracle which accompanies that occasion. There is

nothing here which is necessarily Deuteronomistic, and we can
see no reason to consider it as ill-fitted in its context. It
is true that vs. 31 strikes the reader as something of a concluding sentence, but this need not indicate that vss. 24-31
are a later addition. The verse is proper as the conclusion to
the episode within the chapter of Saul's attempt to mitigate
the judgment, and vs. 32 moves on to the death of Agag. On the
positive side of the argument for the unity of this section
with the rest of the chapter is the clear duplication of the
judgment against Saul in almost identical words in vss. 23 and
26 (ממלך מאסך וימאס יהוה את-דבר מאסת יען, 23; יהוה את-דבר מאסתה כי
על-ישראל מלך מהיות יהוה וימאסך, 26). In the absence of more
positive evidence to the contrary, we find no reason to challenge the literary unity of chapter 15.

The entire chapter is given to a narrative account of the
occasion which led to the rejection of Saul from the kingship.
In the first portion of the chapter (vss. 1-3) Samuel delivers
instructions from Yahweh to Saul that he is to wage holy war
against the Amalekites. This commission is similar to that
given by an unnamed prophet to Ahab in I Kgs. 20:13ff. As here
the prophet makes use of a first-person speech of Yahweh in delivering the commission to the king to fight God's holy war.
The parallel is even more striking in that Ahab, as Saul,
spared the life of the opposing king and was confronted with
the sin by a prophet in an oracle of judgment (I Kgs. 20:35-43).
The speech of Samuel in 15:1-3 is clearly to be considered a
prophetic speech. Its structure might be schematized as follows:

15:1a   Establishment of authority - Samuel recalls his
         previous role as God's messenger in the anointing
         of Saul. He calls special attention to this by
         the emphatic position of אתי. The implication is
         also that the commission which is to follow grows
         out of Saul's role as the anointed one of Yahweh.
    1b   Summons to hear - The introduction of ועתה empha-
         sizes that the claim of the messenger to be heard
         relates to his position as God's messenger estab-
         lished in vs. 1a and supported by his claim to

speak 'the words of the Lord,' דברי יהוה. See
Amos 7:16; Isa. 7:13; and II Kgs. 20:16.

2aα   Messenger formula - כה אמר יהוה צבאות. This is a
well-known introductory formula to prophetic
speech and, as is the case here, is often followed by a first-person speech of Yahweh. Most
noteworthy here is the use of the title יהוה
צבאות which underlines the holy war nature of the
mission given to Saul.[193]

2aβb Pronouncement of Yahweh - Yahweh announces the
coming doom of Amalek. The prophet in I Kgs. 20:
13 also announces the doom of Ben-Hadad's army in
a first-person speech of Yahweh although it makes
use of more explicitly holy war formulae. Here
the doom of Amalek is related to the tradition of
Amalekite opposition to Israel's entry into the
promised land. It is clear that chapter 15 was
not originally connected with the Amalekite reference in 14:48, for there it is simply the fact
that the Amalekites plunder Israel that leads to
Saul's campaign against them. Here Saul is the
instrument of Yahweh's vengeance.

3   The Mission - The use of עתה marks this as the
climactic point of the speech, and Saul is given
the explicit mission to smite (נכה) the Amalekites and put them under the ban (חרם).

It is clear that in vss. 1-3 Samuel is a prophet acting as
God's messenger to send Saul out on a holy war campaign against
the Amalekites. The following section (vss. 4-9) details
Saul's campaign but concludes in vs. 9 that Saul did exactly
what he was commanded not to do. He did not carry out the holy
war ban by destroying all the captives and the spoil (ולא תחמל
עליו, vs. 3; ...-ויחמל שאול והעם על, vs. 9). This preliminary
account of the Amalekite campaign sets the scene for the conflict between Samuel and Saul which leads to Saul's rejection.

The use of ויהי in vs. 10 signals a shift of scene from
the Amalekite war itself to the account of the rejection which
is the point of the chapter. It is clear that in terms of

formal structure we again find the influence of a prophetic
judgment speech directed to an individual although the speech
form itself has been rather thoroughly assimilated into a narrative context as in 13:7b-15a or II Sam. 12. The judgment
speech to an individual has, however, clearly influenced the
shape of the narrative.[194]

Introduction, vss. 1-13 - As we have already mentioned in
our discussion of 13:7b-15a, the introduction is an extremely
variable element in the prophetic speech form. When the speech
form is completely embedded within a narrative setting it tends
to be a more elaborate setting of the scene, giving us the information necessary to understand the cause for judgment which
is about to be pronounced. In this case, all of the introductory material in vss. 1-9 on the mission of Saul and his failure to carry it out completely acts as an introduction to the
judgment which is to come. This is similar to both 13:7b-15a
and II Sam. 12. In chapter 15, however, there is a more immediate introduction than this broad block of narrative background. This is found in the information on the impending
meeting between Samuel and Saul in vss. 10-13. This material
is more immediately introductory to the judgment which follows
although here too the narrator has been quite free in his formulation. That the original prophetic speech form lies behind
this narrative treatment can be seen in vss. 10-11. One of the
most common elements in introductions is the commissioning of
the messenger,[195] and this is characteristically in the form of
a first-person speech by Yahweh (I Kgs. 21:18-19; II Kgs. 1:3-
4). Several matters are made clear by this introductory material. Samuel is the bearer of God's word (ויהי דבר-יהוה
אל-שמואל) which serves to confirm his role here as that of a
prophet. God has already made his judgment on Saul because
Saul has not kept his commandments (ואת-דברי לא הקים). The
scene is clearly one in which Yahweh as judge has rendered a
decision against Saul for the violation of the divine law. It
is Samuel as the prophetic messenger who is to hand down that
decision to the accused.[196] Interestingly, Samuel attempts to
intercede on Saul's behalf, a picture that is difficult to explain for those who would see Samuel as the opponent of Saul

and the kingship. The remaining verses (12-13) simply record
the meeting of Samuel and Saul. By way of dramatic contrast,
Saul is made to greet Samuel by claiming to have done exactly
what God has just pronounced judgment on him for failing to do.

Accusation,[197] vss. 14-21 - The accusation commonly takes
the form of an accusing question (I Sam. 2:29; II Sam. 12:9a;
I Kgs. 21:18; II Kgs. 1:3; Isa. 7:13; 22:16). This accusing
question can be distinguished here in vs. 14 ומה קול-הצאן הזה
באזני וקול הבקר אשר אנכי שמע, "What is this bleating of the
sheep in my ears and the lowing of the cattle which I hear?"
As already seen in 13:11 (cf. also II Kgs. 20:14f.), this is a
case where the question is not clearly explicit as to the nature of the transgression, but as pointed out earlier the entire process of directing questions which are answered by the
accused is similar to a judicial hearing in which the nature of
the transgression is established.[198] This is certainly appli-
cable to chapter 15. Saul's answer to Samuel's accusing question clearly establishes that the holy war ban has not been
carried out. It is interesting in this connection that Saul
uses the third person in speaking of those things which were
not destroyed but shifts to the first person in speaking of the
portion of the spoil which was destroyed. Some have interpreted this as an attempt by Saul to shift the blame, which recalls the use of the emphatic pronoun in 13:11. In vss. 17-21,
it would seem that the hearing continues. In vss. 17-18, we
find an example of a contrast motif commonly found in the prophetic judgment speech, I Sam. 2:30; 13:13f.; II Sam. 12:7b-9;
I Kgs. 14:7f., 10. "The motif here contrasts the offense of
which the party is accused with the fact that he has been installed in his office by Yahweh and has been the recipient of
other beneficial deeds. Behind this frequently recurring motif, there must be an old motif that belongs to the accusation
speech of the prophets."[199] In 15:17ff., Saul is reminded that
he holds his office by virtue of Yahweh's anointment. He is
further reminded that he was sent on a mission of holy war
against the Amalekites. These are set in contrast to Saul's
behaviour which is reintroduced in another series of accusing
questions in vs. 19, "Why then did you not obey the voice of

the Lord? Why did you swoop on the spoil, and do what was evil
in the sight of the Lord?" Saul's basic transgression is that
of disobedience. In a continuation of the hearing procedure,
Saul answers by denying that he has not obeyed the voice of
Yahweh, but in the process he reveals to Samuel that he has
spared the life of Agag the king of the Amalekites. He further
attempts to justify the failure to carry out the ban by claiming that the best of the spoils were saved to be sacrificed to
Yahweh at Gilgal. Interestingly, it is the people who are made
the originators of this idea. The cross-examination type of
procedure exhibited by the accusing questions and the answers
of the accused have effectively fulfilled their purpose and established the facts of the transgression which Saul has commit-
ted and for which he has been judged by Yahweh.

Oracle, vss. 22-23 - In contrast to the rest of the chapter, these verses are poetry rather than prose. They stand at
the climactic point of the chapter where Saul's guilt has been
established and the judgment is awaited. Thus, it is at the
junction of accusation and announcement in the narrative. A
closer look at the oracle shows that it contains within itself
both accusation and announcement, and thus serves as a link between the two parts of the narrative. In vs. 22a we find the
accusatory question which immediately identifies the nature of
Saul's transgression as disobedience. The accusation is expanded in vss. 22b-23a by a positive statement of the greater
worth of obedience than cultic observance (vs. 22b) and an
equation of disobedience with divination and idolatry (i.e.
apostasy, vs. 23a). This is a common prophetic theme found
also in Isa. 1; Amos 5; Jer. 7; and Hos. 6. In vs. 23b, a
straightforward declaratory accusation is made, מאסת את-דבר
יהוה. We have noticed the word מאס before as common in prophetic speech as a description of the refusal of God's will (8:7;
10:19). The most interesting aspect of vs. 23b, however, is
that it is begun with the particle יען, thus bringing the accusation into a logical-grammatical connection with the announcement which follows, וימאסך ממלך. This is in contrast to
the original form of the speech which simply juxtaposes the
two parts without stating a causal relationship. The oracle,

therefore, represents a relatively late development in the form. This causal relationship was also noted in I Sam. 13:14. In content, the oracle also shows evidence of a tendency to state the accusation in general, conceptual terms (disobedience) rather than the earlier accusations which focus on a single particular violation of God's law (cf. I Kgs. 20:36; II Kgs. 21:11). To be sure, the particular violation is still preserved in the narrative which surrounds the oracle, but it might be regarded as a development in the direction of an accusation stated completely in general conceptual terms. Westermann writes in this regard: "Within this form we can therefore recognize the clear features of a history of the prophetic accusation directed to an individual. Its course goes from the accusation which is issued in a single completely isolated sentence (a declaration or accusing question) to one that is causally connected with the announcement; in regard to content, this goes from an accusation that establishes a single definite transgression to one that is generally and conceptually formulated."[200] A further feature common in the prophetic judgment speech to an individual is the correspondence between the punishment announced and the accusation made. There seems to be a conscious attempt to show the punishment as appropriate to the transgression (I Sam. 2:29, 32; II Sam. 12:7-11; I Kgs. 20:42; II Kgs. 20:17). Although it seems to be a regular feature of the speech form, the origin and meaning of this motif remain unknown.[201] Thus, we can see that the brief oracle in vss. 22-23 is in itself a complete example of the prophetic speech form under discussion. It may well be that it is around this speech that the narrative was constructed since it neatly divides between the accusation and the announcement in the narrative. Such a question, however, is impossible to answer.

Announcement, vss. 24-31 - We view this portion of the narrative as dominated by the announcement since its concern is wholly with the judgment pronounced against Saul and his attempt to mitigate its harshness. The initial announcement was made in the oracle in vs. 23b so that this portion of the narrative opens with Saul's confession. He admits to the sin he had previously denied in vs. 13 and attributes it to his fear

of the people. A confession is a well-known way of attempting
to soften judgments in the Old Testament,[202] but here it is to
no avail. The judgment has already been rendered by Yahweh,
and Samuel is simply the messenger delivering this judgment.
Yahweh has repented (נחם) of his decision to make Saul king,
and from this judgment there is no appeal as is already illus-
trated by the failure of Samuel's intercession (vs. 11). Thus,
Samuel can only respond to Saul's confession by a reiteration
of the announcement made in vs. 23b in virtually the same words
in vs. 26. Nothing new is added to the judgment in this repetition. However, in vss. 27-29, the announcement is carried
further by means of a sign. A large number of the examples of
the prophetic judgment speech to an individual have a connection between the announcement and a sign, and Westermann has
emphasized that these signs are always connected to the announcement and never to the accusation.[203] Examples are found
in I Sam. 2:34; II Sam. 12:14; I Kgs. 11:30f.; 13:3; 14:12;
Isa. 7:14; 37:30f. The question of the origin and nature of
prophetic signs lies outside the scope of our study, but it is
clear that they appear as a regular part of the prophetic
speech of judgment to individuals, and need not be considered
a sign of late authorship. In 15:27-29, the sign is a dramatic
tearing of Samuel's robe by Saul, and it provides an occasion
for a further announcement of judgment. Using the tearing
image which has presented itself, Samuel announces, "The Lord
has torn the kingdom of Israel from you this day, and has given
it to a neighbor of yours who is better than you." This is
clearly a reference to David who is to be anointed in the following chapter and later assumes the kingship. It should be
remembered that in 13:14 the denial of dynasty to Saul was also
linked with the future blessing to be given to David. The final verse of Samuel's speech (29) only serves to emphasize the
irrevocable nature of Yahweh's judgment in this matter, a point
already made earlier in the chapter as well. Saul does confess
his sin again despite this statement, but he does not ask as
before to be forgiven for his sin. He asks only that Samuel
honor him before the people, and this Samuel can agree to do.

Just a brief word might be added on the nature of the
punishment assessed here against Saul. Here Saul is actually

rejected as king. In effect, the office which was bestowed
upon him by the anointing (which is referred to twice in this
chapter, vss. 1, 17, as the basis for Saul's accession to the
throne) is revoked. In 16:13, which immediately follows our
account, David becomes the anointed of Yahweh and receives the
spirit of Yahweh just as Saul did following his anointment. It
cannot be accidental that 16:14 records that the spirit of Yahweh left Saul and was replaced by an evil spirit. This cannot
be other than the consequence of the rejection in chapter 15.
By way of contrast, we can recall the account of 13:7b-15a.
There Saul was only cut off from the possibility of dynasty,
and there is no evidence that this was considered to have any
effect on the continued performance of his kingly role. The
effects of the two judgments directed against Saul are thus
quite different. We shall return to this question again shortly.

The remainder of the chapter is uncomplicated. In vss.
32-33, Samuel carries out the instructions given to Saul concerning the utter destruction of the spoil by killing Agag,
apparently in the sanctuary at Gilgal. The attempt by Agag to
suggest that the whole matter be cheerfully forgotten stands in
stark contrast to the unswerving carrying out of the holy war
ban by Samuel. The brief speech of Samuel is in effect an accusation and announcement directed to Agag with Samuel actually
carrying out the punishment pronounced. This role of the
prophet is without parallel.

Vss. 34-35, recording the return to their homes by Samuel
and Saul, are simply the closing notes to the account. However, there is the interesting note that Samuel grieved (התאבל)
over Saul. This would certainly mitigate against considering
this chapter as unconscionably anti-Saul. The final comment is
a doublet of vs. 11 and ends the narrative on the already emphasized note of the irrevocability of God's judgment.

From our discussion of its form and content, it is not
hard to identify the setting in which the tradition of chapter
15 was preserved as that of early prophetic circles concerned
to explain Saul's rejection as king as due to his disobedience
to God's word. As we have already noted above,[204] the judgment

speech to individuals had its proper time before the period of prophetic activity. It has been mentioned that there is some evidence that chapter 15 represents an example of later development in the form. The causal relation of accusation and announcement in vs. 23 and the tendency to state the transgression in general conceptual form are both later developments in the judgment speech to individuals. Indeed, the general similarities in the theme of the oracle in vss. 22-23 to oracles in the early writing prophets might also stand as evidence that our chapter in its present form stands near the junction between the period of early prophecy and that of the writing prophets. This should not, however, mislead us into concluding that chapter 15 stems completely from a late time in the period of the writing prophets (or from a late Deuteronomistic hand). The role of Samuel, the view of the king and the concern for obedience to God's word are all presented in terms consistent with the traditions of the early prophets. Samuel appears here as a clearly prophetic figure. He identifies himself in vs. 1 as the one commissioned by Yahweh to anoint Saul king; he delivers the commission to wage holy war against the Amalekites, and when the holy war ban is not fulfilled he is the messenger of Yahweh who delivers judgment on Saul for his failure to obey the divine word. These functions are well attested for the early prophets, and cannot apply to any other functionary of the period. For example, in II Sam. 12, Nathan confronts David with his transgression in a manner similar to Samuel in chapter 15. He appeals to the anointment of David (12:7) and moves to indict him for despising the word of Yahweh (12:9). An even closer parallel to the role of Samuel in chapter 15 can be seen in the unknown prophet who sends Ahab into holy war against Ben-Hadad and then pronounces judgment against him for failing to carry out the ban in killing Ben-Hadad (I Kgs. 20:13ff.). Certainly the role of Samuel supports the prophetic provenance of chapter 15.

We must now turn to the question of the relationship of chapter 15 to the other materials in I Sam. 7-15. The most obvious question to raise is that of connections between the two rejection stories (13:7b-15a and 15). It is possible that the

two accounts are merely variants of the same event. It is
striking that both occur at Gilgal and that both involve a
judgment against Saul by Samuel for a violation of the sacral
regulations surrounding the holy war. These similarities may
well be due to the common origin of the accounts in the same
event, a conflict between Samuel and Saul at Gilgal. In any
case, the two accounts now appear in quite different contexts
and serve different functions. In 13:7b-15a, the context is
the Philistine war, and Saul's transgression involves some now
obscure violation of the ritual of sacrifice which precedes the
holy war. The function of the pericope is apparently to account for the fact that Saul's dynasty was not established
whereas David's was. In chapter 15, the context is a holy war
proclaimed against the Amalekites in which Saul fails to carry
out the ban and spares Agag and some of the best of the spoils.
Here the function is to account for Saul's rejection from the
kingship, apparently in order to make intelligible the anointing of a new king and the departure of the spirit from Saul in
chapter 16. The differences in the two accounts, however, cannot be explained by the hypothesis that they were preserved in
completely different circles.[205] In formal structure, we have
seen that both are very similar in that they show the influence of the prophetic judgment speech to an individual. Furthermore, both show this form in a rather late stage of development which links the accusation and announcement causally and
states the transgression in the more general, conceptual manner
as disobedience to God's word or commandment. In content, it
is also noteworthy that Saul's failure is in both coupled with
an intimation of David's future success. Little can be said
about the origin of these two accounts (e.g. whether they stem
from the same event or not), but it is clear that in their
present form they have been shaped by the same circles. These
circles have been identified as those of the early prophets
prior to the period of the writing prophets. If these two accounts then stem from the same setting, they cannot be considered as doublets, but serve two different purposes. In their
present context, they act as the answers to two related but
separate questions: Why was Saul rejected as king and David

chosen before the death of Saul, and why was Saul's dynasty not established forever while David's was? The answer to both was that Saul failed the test of obedience to God's word and was judged guilty and punished. As we shall argue in greater detail in the conclusion, this is a further element in the organizing principle of the career of the anointed. He who would be God's anointed must stand the test. David is the one who does stand the test, and his innocence is emphasized in the David-Saul material (I Sam. 19:4-5; 20:1, 8; 24:4-22; 25:32-34; 26: 8-25; 27:8-11; 29:4ff.; 30:17ff., 23ff.). Knierim has recognized this element when he states, "Saul fails in the testing and is rejected, David does not fail in the testing and is therefore finally confirmed (II Sam. 7)."[206] This outcome is already foreshadowed in the judgments pronounced in both chapters 13 and 15.

As previously mentioned, many scholars have seen chapter 15 as a continuation of chapter 12. This is generally supported on the basis of the assertion that the rejection of Saul is the culmination of the anti-monarchical sentiment expressed in the so-called late source. There is, however, no direct evidence of a connection between chapter 15 and the chapters usually placed in the late source. Further, Weiser has already stressed the point that the attitude toward Saul in this chapter can by no means be considered simply negative.[207]

Hertzberg[208] has argued that chapter 15 was originally connected to 11. As support for this hypothesis, he notes that neither chapter mentions the Philistines, both involve Gilgal, Samuel is with Saul in both, and 15:4 is reminiscent of 11:8. None of these points, however, will support the hypothesis. The absence of the mention of the Philistines does not argue for a relationship. If it did, one might claim that since chapter 11 does not mention Amalekites and chapter 15 does not mention Ammonites the evidence is just as strong against a relationship. Gilgal is the locus only for the final ceremony in chapter 11, and in any case, topography does not prove relationship. Further, we have previously shown that it is doubtful that the brief reference to Samuel in chapter 11 can be considered original, and 15:4 and 11:8 are simply examples of

the numbering procedure which is often described in connection
with military accounts. It seems highly unlikely that chapters
11 and 15 were originally connected, although both may play a
role in a larger framework.

The most likely connection of chapter 15 to earlier material would seem to be a relation to the account of Saul's
anointing in 9:1-10:16. There seems to be an obvious reference
to Samuel's anointing of Saul (10:1) in 15:1, and the anointing
is referred to again in vs. 17. It is appropriate that in delivering the command to wage holy war against the Amalekites,
Samuel refers to the anointing since in 10:1 Saul's specific
mission as Yahweh's anointed is to "save them (Israel) from the
hand of their enemies round about." It would almost seem that
9:1-10:16 and chapter 15 serve to chronicle the beginning and
end of Saul's career as God's anointed. We have already noted
that both accounts are heavily influenced by prophetic forms
(call narrative and judgment speech), and in their present
shape, they may well stem from prophetic circles of the same
general period. As a further support to this connection, it is
possible that Samuel's remark in 15:17 refers back to Saul's
disclaimer in 9:21.

* * *

We may summarize our conclusions on chapter 15 as follows:
The entire narrative has been influenced by the form of
the prophetic judgment speech to an individual. The particular
elements of this formal type that can be noted in the chapter
show that I Sam. 15 seems to represent a somewhat late stage in
the development of the form since it shows the causal connection between accusation and announcement. The role of Samuel,
the interest in holy war and the concern for obedience to God's
word are all consistent with the interests of early prophetic
circles, and the tradition in its present form probably stems
from prophetic circles to be dated near the start of the period
of the 8th century classical prophets. These are probably the
same circles responsible for the present shape of 13:7b-15a,
and the two traditions are not to be considered doublets but
serve two quite distinct purposes. The one explains the failure of Saul to establish a dynasty, and the other explains the

rejection of Saul as king and the subsequent withdrawal of the spirit from him. Because of the reference to Saul's anointment by Samuel in the chapter and the influence of clearly identifiable prophetic forms in both, chapter 15 may be said to be linked to the account of Saul's anointment in 9:1-10:16. Evidence is lacking for any direct links with other material in I Sam. 7-15.

NOTES

CHAPTER II

[1]Smith, *A Critical and Exegetical Commentary on the Books of Samuel*, pp. xviff.; Pfeiffer, *Introduction to the Old Testament*, pp. 359ff.; Muilenburg, *Tell En-Nasbeh*, edited by C. C. McCown (New Haven, 1947), pp. 23ff.; Eissfeldt, *The Old Testament: An Introduction*, pp. 271f., places it in his E source.

[2]G. B. Caird, "The First and Second Books of Samuel," *The Interpreter's Bible*, vol. 2 (Nashville: Abingdon Press, 1953), pp. 913ff.; Kennedy, *Samuel*, *The New Century Bible*, pp. 23ff. Wellhausen was the first to claim Deuteronomic affinities for this chapter; see *Prolegomena to the History of Ancient Israel*, pp. 245-272.

[3]Noth, *Überlieferungsgeschichtliche Studien*, pp. 54ff.

[4]Artur Weiser, "Samuels 'Philister-Sieg': Die Überlieferungen in I Samuel 7," *ZThK*, 56 (1959), 253ff., and *Samuel: Seine geschichtliche Aufgabe und religiöse Bedeutung*.

[5]Martin Buber, "Die Erzählung von Sauls Königswahl," *VT*, 6 (1956), 113ff., suggests that old traditions lie in vss. 5-11, 15-17 and vss. 3-4, 13-14 are added by a later editor. The aetiological note in vs. 12 was attached to 5-11 before this final editor. Horst Seebass, "Traditionsgeschichte von I Sam. 8, 10:17ff. und 12," *ZAW*, 77 (1965), pp. 286ff., follows Buber essentially but sees 5-12 as the combination of a tradition relating a penance ceremony (vss. 2, 5-6, 8-9) and a tradition of Yahweh's miraculous victory (vss. 7, 10-12).

[6]See Noth, *op. cit.*, for a representative treatment.

[7]I Sam. 7:1 belongs with the history of the ark in 4:1b-7:1 and will not concern us here.

[8]Noth, *op. cit.*, pp. 18ff.

[9]James Muilenburg, *Tell En-Nasbeh*, edited by C. C. McCown, pp. 23ff., and "Mizpah of Benjamin," *StTh*, 8 (1955), pp. 25-42. He argues that Mizpah is not known as a sanctuary until post-exilic times and its appearance in Jdgs. 20-21, I Sam. 7 and 10 is a late addition to the text. He feels this is shown by the appearance of Mizpah only in places clearly of an editorial nature.

[10]Seebass' view (see n. 5) that vss. 7, 10-12 belong with the victory tradition but vss. 8-9 belong to the penance tradition cannot be supported. The mention of the offering in vs. 10 shows that it must be read with vs. 9, and the people's request in vs. 8 makes little sense without the notice of impending danger in vs. 7. Syntactically the narrative in vss. 7-11 reads smoothly and there is no reason to consider it as a composite account.

[11] James Muilenburg, "The Form and Structure of the Covenantal Formulations," *VT*, 9 (1959), pp. 354-55. To be sure, this is an incomplete example of the *Gattung* with which Muilenburg is dealing.

[12] It should be noted, however, that the combination of apodictic commands with result clauses expressing the benefits of fulfillment is extremely characteristic of the parenetic framework of Deuteronomy (e.g. 6:18; 8:1; 11:8). In Deuteronomy the command is usually in the indicative rather than imperative as here. As we shall note later, the concern for purity of Yahweh worship which is shown in I Sam. 7:3-4 is also a well known concern of Deuteronomy.

[13] E. Nielsen, "The Burial of the Foreign Gods," *StTh*, 8 (1955), pp. 103ff., and *Shechem: A Traditio-Historical Investigation* (Copenhagen: G.E.C. Gad, 1954), pp. 234ff. He argues from comparative Near Eastern evidence for a rather complicated development of this ritual in Israel, but the Near Eastern evidence is too diverse and the Old Testament evidence too limited for his conclusions. We are persuaded, however, that the formula of putting aside foreign gods in Gen. 35:1-4 is related to the terror of Yahweh in vs. 5. This would suggest a relation of the formula to holy war concepts. Perhaps the setting is the purification which precedes holy war. This could well have involved cultic purity and would explain the explicit combination of the formula with the concern for purity of Yahwistic worship in Jos. 24:23; Jdgs. 10:16; and I Sam. 7:3. The use of the formula in Gen. 35:2 probably represents an earlier stage when a ritual "putting-away" of foreign gods was considered directly responsible for annihilation of enemies similar to the execration figures from Egypt adduced by Nielsen as parallels.

[14] Against A. L. Merrill, *I Sam. 1-12: A Traditio-Historical Study*, Univ. of Chicago Dissertation, 1962, pp. 123ff. He draws the following comparison:

	I Sam. 7	Gen. 35
a. Call to put away the gods	3-4	2-3
b. Purification of the people	5-6	4
c. Terror on the enemies	10-11	5
d. Building of altar	17	7
e. Setting up pillar	12	14-15

Such a comparison ignores the composite nature of I Sam. 7 and represents only rough similarities in motif. There are no literary or form critical similarities, and Merrill's comparison cannot be taken seriously.

[15] This line of research was begun by A. Alt, "Die Wallfahrt von Sichem nach Bethel," *Kleine Schriften zur Geschichte des Volkes Israel*, vol. I (München: C. H. Beck, 1959), pp. 79ff. (original article published 1938)

[16] See G. von Rad, *Deuteronomy* (Philadelphia: Westminster Press, 1966). It should be noted that in Deuteronomy itself passages concerned with cultic purity generally use the term אלהים אחרים rather than אלהי הנכר. The use of the two phrases, however, seems closely analogous.

[17] On Jos. 24 see Eissfeldt, *Introduction*, p. 255. Although scholars disagree on the relationship of Jos. 23 and 24, most agree that Jos. 24 shows evidence of Deuteronomistic editing of older tradition material while 23 is probably a complete composition by a Deuteronomistic hand. Jos. 24:23-24 must be regarded as one of the points showing the Deuteronomistic hand. On Jdgs. 10:6-16, see W. Richter, *Die Bearbeitungen des "Retterbuches" in der deuteronomischen Epoche* (Bonn: Peter Hanstein, 1964), pp. 13ff.

[18] Deut. 4:29; 6:5; 10:12; 11:13; 13:4; 26:16; 30:2,6,10; Jos. 22:5; 23:14; I Sam. 12:24; Jer. 29:13; Joel 2:12. In Deuteronomy this phrase is usually accompanied by the phrase "and with all your soul."

[19] See J. Pedersen, *Israel: Its Life and Culture*, vol. 2 (London: Oxford University Press, 1926), pp. 243, 424, 517, 520, 750, for the references on water libations and their meaning in later rites.

[20] The formula of congregational confession also appears in a Deuteronomistic context in Jdgs. 10:10-15 in close connection to the themes which were compared earlier to I Sam. 7:3-4. This might seem to suggest that vss. 3-4 and 6 are both from the same Deuteronomistic hand. The congregational confession also appears in what is generally regarded as a Deuteronomistic context in Deut. 1:41 and I Sam. 12:10. However, it appears as well in an older tradition context in Num 14:40; 21:7 (both JE). A closer examination of I Sam. 7:3-4, 6 excludes any original relationship. The return to Yahweh from apostasy is recorded as accomplished with no reservations in 7:4. The confession of sin in vs. 6 hardly makes any sense following vs. 4. One can only conclude that the Deuteronomist who added 7:3-4 found the tradition of vs. 6 already in its present position, although it is possible that the presence of a congregational confession in the material before him may have influenced his decision to place a brief introduction similar to Jdgs. 10:6-16 at this place.

[21] See R. de Vaux, *Ancient Israel: Its Life and Institutions* (London: Darton, Longman and Todd, 1961), pp. 258ff.

[22] Jos. 10:10; Jdgs. 4:15; I Sam. 7:10; II Sam. 22:15//Ps. 18:14. This last instance is technically the description of Yahweh's theophany but in this context Yahweh appears as warrior routing his enemies. This is the cosmic dimension of holy war which parallels the earthly dimension. Cf. F. Cross, "The Divine Warrior in Israel's Early Cult," *Biblical Motifs*, Alexander Altmann, editor (Cambridge: Harvard Univ. Press, 1966), pp. 11ff.

[23] W. Richter, *Traditionsgeschichtliche Untersuchungen zum Richterbuch* (Bonn: Peter Hanstein, 1963), p. 181. The other schema is represented in our material in I Sam. 11 and will be discussed there.

[24] We can see no reason to consider vs. 12 as secondary (as do many scholars) simply because the name Eben-ha-'ezer appears also in 4:1 and 5:2. There are no literary or form-critical grounds for separating vs. 12, and there are many instances of different places possessing the same name. The double appearance of the name does not require that one be claimed as inauthentic.

[25] R. Bach, *Die Aufforderungen zur Flucht und zum Kampf im alttestamentlichen Prophetenspruch* (Neukirchen: Neukirchener Verlag, 1962), p. 112.

[26] R. Rendtorff, "Reflections on the Early History of Prophecy in Israel," *History and Hermeneutic* (New York: Harper and Row, 1967), p. 28 (translated by Paul Achtemeier from an article in *ZThK*, 59 [1962], pp. 145-67).

[27] Mention should be made of H. Seebass' hypothesis (see reference in n. 5) that I Sam. 7:5-12 is parallel in structure to 12:16-25. He charts the following similarities:

		7:5	12:16a
1.	Call to position	7:5	12:16a
2.	Samuel as a man through whom Yahweh works	7:10	12:16-18
3.	God's voice	7:10	12:17,18
4.	Confession of sin	7:6	12:19b
5.	Request not to cease intercession	7:8	12:19a,23a
6.	Stereotyped decision point	7:3-4	12:20,23b,24

Close examination hardly allows us to take his suggestion seriously. There is no similarity of order to the listed elements in the two passages, and the elements are often totally dissimilar in the two passages. For example, the motif of God's voice קול in I Sam. 7:10 has been shown to be part of a holy war schema. In 12:17,18, קול is being used simply to indicate thunder, and the context seems to be the giving of a prophetic sign. It is not designated there as God's voice. The similarity in motif 5 consists only in the appearance of the verb חרש in both passages. The other motifs fare little better on close examination, and the hypothesis seems to have little to recommend itself.

[28] B. Long, *The Problem of Etiological Narrative in the Old Testament*, BZAW 107 (Berlin: Töpelmann, 1968), p. 36.

[29] Jdgs. 3:30; 8:28; 11:33; I Chron. 20:4. The verb also appears in the hiphil in Jdgs. 4:23.

[30] Deut. 2:15; Jdgs. 2:15; I Sam. 12:15. As we shall see later, I Sam. 12 probably shows the influence of a Deuteronomistic hand. The construction also appears in I Sam. 5:9 which cannot be considered Deuteronomistic.

[31] See S. R. Driver, *A Critical and Exegetical Commentary on Deuteronomy*, ICC (Edinburgh: T. & T. Clark, 1895), pp. 11-12, for a detailed discussion of the use of Amorite and Canaanite in the Pentateuch. His mention of the tendency in D to limit Canaanite to the inhabitants of the seacoast and the

Jordan Valley while using Amorite for all the rest of the pre-Israelite populace accords well with I Sam. 7:14. The Philistines (seacoast people) have been dealt with in vs. 13 and the final note in vs. 14 is to imply that peace was enjoyed with all the rest of the non-Israelite populace.

[32]Rendtorff, *History and Hermeneutic*, pp. 30-31. M. Noth, "Office and Vocation in the Old Testament," *The Laws in the Pentateuch and Other Studies*, translated by D. R. Ap-Thomas (Edinburgh: Oliver and Boyd, 1966), pp. 242ff.

[33]Wellhausen, *Prolegomena*, pp. 245-72; Smith, *Books of Samuel*, ICC, pp. xviiff.; Pfeiffer, *Introduction*, p. 360; Driver, *Introduction*, pp. 175f.; Caird, *I and II Samuel*, IB, vol. 2. Eissfeldt, *Introduction*, pp. 271ff., places I Sam. 8 in his E source.

[34]Noth, *Überlieferungsgeschichtliche Studien*, pp. 56-57.

[35]Artur Weiser, "Samuel und die Vorgeschichte des israelitischen Konigtums," *ZThK*, 57 (1960), 141-61; and *Samuel* (see n. 4). See H. W. Hertzberg, *I and II Samuel* (Philadelphia: Westminster Press, 1964), for a similar view.

[36]See note 35.

[37]It also appears in Jos. 23:16; 24:2, 16; ten times in the framework to I and II Kings and eighteen times in Jeremiah which has often been cited for its similarity in language to Deuteronomy. See Richter, *Die Bearbeitungen*, pp. 58-59, for a detailed discussion.

[38]*Ibid.*, pp. 28, 58ff. Richter points out that Jdgs. 2: 11, 12, 13; 10:6, 11; and I Sam. 12:10 all use proper names rather than the general אלהים אחרים used in I Sam. 8:8, but both are Deuteronomistic.

[39]The following schematization shows the formal structure of the unit:

יקח	11 את בניכם
	ושם לו במרכבתו ובפרשיו ורצו לפני מרכבתו
	12 ולשום לו שרי אלפים ושרי חמשים
	ולחרש חרישו ולקצר קצירו
	ולעשות כלי-מלחמתו וכלי רכבו
יקח	13 ואת בנותכם
	לרקחות
	ולטבחות
	ולאפות
יקח	14 ואת שדותיכם ואת כרמיכם וזיתיכם הטובים
	ונתן לעבדיו
יעשר	15 וזרעיכם וכרמיכם
	ונתן לסריסיו ולעבדיו
יקח	16 ואת עבדיכם ואת שפחותיכם ואת בחוריכם הטובים ואת חמוריכם
	ועשה למלאכתו
יעשר	17 צאנכם
	ואתם תהיו לו לעבדים

Note the unusual recurring pattern of object-verb word order with
with repeated use of לקח and עשׂר. Merrill, *I Sam. 1-12: A
Traditio-historical Study*, pp. 134-45, has suggested that this
unit really represents a compilation of two types of formulae,
one using לקח and the other עשׂר. This view would be strength-
ened by the observation that vss. 14 and 15 represent a doublet. Each uses a different formula to express the same result,
the giving of property to the king's servants. There is little
reason, however, to doubt that the unit 11-17 was substantially
in its present form when it was brought into chapter 8.

[40] I. Mendelsohn, "Samuel's Denunciation of Kingship in the
Light of Akkadian Documents from Ugarit," *BASOR*, 143 (1956),
17-22.

[41] H. Seebass, *ZAW*, 77 (1965), pp. 286ff.

[42] The phrase is translated in 8:9 as "ways of the king"
and in 10:25 as "rights and duties of the kingship."

[43] Even Noth, *Überlieferungsgeschichtliche Studien*, pp.
56-7, agrees that this is an old tradition although he attributes the rest of the chapter to the Deuteronomist.

[44] The reference here to a southern sanctuary (Beer-sheba)
has seemed problematic to some. However, we have already seen
in I Sam. 7 that both the Deuteronomistic hand (7:3) and an
earlier hand (7:5) stressed the all-Israel character of Samuel's leadership. Perhaps the notice here shows that this
stress has some basis in fact. It is at least interesting to
note that Beer-sheba appears in close connection with the
northern cult centers of Bethel, Gilgal and Dan in Amos 5:5
and 8:14.

[45] Note that in the elders' speech in vs. 5 the emphatic
construction using the reinforcing pronoun אתה and placing the
subject prior to the verb has the effect of emphasizing the
elimination of all possibilities except that of a king. This
possibility is then forcefully introduced by the particle עתה
indicating the climactic point of the elders' speech.

[46] See note 35.

[47] In vs. 8, the formula עד-היום הזה is used with מן to
indicate the *terminus ad quem* of a temporal sequence. The
clause should be read as frequentative indicating the continued
apostasy of Israel. See Brevard S. Childs, "A Study of the
Formula, 'Until this day'," *JBL*, 82 (1963), pp. 279ff. This is
in contrast to vs. 7 which lacks this frequentative emphasis.

[48] See W. Schmidt, *Königtum Gottes in Ugarit und Israel*,
BZAW, 80 (Berlin: A. Töpelmann, 1961).

[49] Smith, *Books of Samuel*, *ICC*, pp. xviiiff.; Driver,
Introduction, p. 175; Pfeiffer, *Introduction*, pp. 344ff.;
Caird, *I and II Samuel*, *IB*, vol. 2, p. 857; Eissfeldt, *Intro-
duction*, p. 275, places this section in his J source.

[50]Weiser, *The Old Testament: Its Formation and Development*, pp. 157-69, stresses the diverse origins of the materials in 9:1-10:16; 11; 13-14, but still views them as having come together in a collection of materials on the rise of Saul before the formation of I Samuel as we now have it. Klaus-Dietrich Schunck, *Benjamin*, BZAW, 86 (Berlin: Alfred Töpelmann, 1963), treats these as a Jabesh-Gilgal source made up of a Jabesh tradition (11) and a Gilgal tradition (9:1-10:16; 13:1-14:46).

[51]Hugo Gressmann, *Die Schriften des Alten Testaments*, II, no. 1, pp. 26ff.

[52]Hertzberg, *I and II Samuel*, pp. 75ff. Although disagreeing on some of the particulars, Georg Fohrer, "Der Vertrag zwischen König und Volk in Israel," *ZAW*, 71 (1959), pp. 1-22, and H. Wildberger, "Samuel und die Entstehung des israelitischen Königtums," *Theologische Zeitschrift*, 13 (1957), pp. 442ff., also view 9:1-10:16 as the combination of originally independent traditions combined before incorporation into larger frameworks.

[53]H. Seebass, "Die Vorgeschichte der Königserhebung Sauls," *ZAW*, 79 (1967), pp. 155ff., feels the section can be completely divided into two originally independent traditions, one a story of Saul's youth and the other an account of his anointing.

[54]Richter, *Traditionsgeschichtliche Untersuchungen zum Richterbuch*, p. 13, refers to the construction ויהי איש as "einer allgemeiner Floskel." It might also be here noted that I am indebted to Richter for the assertion that both of these introductory formulae may be taken as characteristic of a narrative style although I had distinguished the differences in the formulae independently of his work.

[55]See note 51, above. W. A. Irwin, "Samuel and the Rise of the Monarchy," *AJSL*, 58 (1941), p. 120, notes, however, that Gressmann was anticipated in this conclusion by Eichhorn.

[56]Adolphe Lods, *Israel from its Beginnings to the Middle of the Eighth Century*, p. 353.

[57]There have been several recent advocates of a symbolic interpretation of the search for the lost asses.
M. Bič, "Saul sucht die Eselinnen (I Sam. 9)," *VT*, 7 (1957), pp. 92-7, sees a Canaanite cultic background to the story. It reflects a ritual search of the four sides of the world. Zuph stands for honey as the symbol of paradise; Shalisha is the number three, symbolic of resurrection on the third day; and Sha'alim is the jackal head of Anubis, goddess of the underworld. Saul's search is thus given cosmic dimension as the search for a rising deity and the climax of the ritual re-enactment of this search is the triumphal entry of a young man sitting on an ass. This can hardly be considered a plausible view. It rests heavily on the interpretation of the place names in 9:4 as cultic symbols, a view for which there is

no independent evidence. Further, there is no evidence of a triumphal entry; Saul does not ride an ass at any time in the story and in fact does not himself find the lost asses--they are found while he is away.

H. J. Stoebe, "Noch einmal die Eselinnen des Kiš," *VT*, 7 (1957), pp. 362-70, attempts to relate this section to the call and anointing of David. His most interesting observation in this regard is the fact that David comes to Saul's court with an ass, bread, a skin of wine, and a kid (cf. 10:2-4). Stoebe sees this as provisions for a young warrior; hence, both 10:2-4 and 16:20 reflect the mission of Saul and David to deliver Israel. Hertzberg, *I and II Samuel*, p. 141, rightly objects that this reading of 16:10 ignores the fact that David is coming to Saul as a musician, not a soldier. The items are probably to be seen as gifts even though it is possible that the author of this pericope consciously chose these gifts in ironic imitation of the well-known story of Saul as a youth.

A. L. Merrill, *I Sam. 1-12: A Traditio-historical Study*, pp. 145ff., sees Saul's search for the asses as a search for the kingship since asses are known elsewhere to have royal significance (Gen. 49:11; Jdgs. 5:10; 10:4; 12:14; I Kgs. 1:33; Zech. 9:9). However, there is a pointed absence of any mention of kingship in 9:1-10:16, and asses are so well known in contexts other than those of royal motifs that Merrill's conclusion seems based on evidence so slender as to make it implausible.

[58]I. Hylander, *Der literarische Samuel-Saul-Komplex (I Sam. 1-15)*, (Uppsala: Almqvist and Wiksell, 1932), pp. 139ff., argues that the change from 'man of God,' אִישׁ אלחים, in 9:6-8, 10 to 'seer,' ראה, in 9:11-13 indicates that there were two originally independent sources which have been conflated here. Vs. 9:9a is intended as a transition from 'man of God' to 'seer' and 9b was added later to connect the seer with Samuel. Such a view would be more persuasive if 9:9 coincided with a literary seam in the narrative, but it clearly breaks the flow of an otherwise stylistically smooth text. Vs. 9:9 must be read as an insertion made after 9:1-13 was already in its present form. In that case there is little reason not to see the entire verse as intended to explain why Samuel, the prophet, is referred to as a seer. The writer is obviously speaking from a time when one went to prophets to inquire of God, and he is assuring his readers that in earlier days these men were sometimes called seers.

[59]H. Seebass, "Die Vorgeschichte der Königserhebung Sauls," *ZAW*, 97 (1967), pp. 155ff., argues for a division of sources in 9:22-24. He feels that the thirty guests of vs. 22 conflict with the phrase העם קראתי in vs. 24 which indicates to Seebass a public feast. Vs. 23 and the phrase למועד שמור לך in vs. 24 show for Seebass that Saul received specially prepared pieces, and this is in conflict with the statement הנה הנשאר שים לפניך in vs. 24 which indicates that Saul received leftovers. This is slender evidence on which to make a clear division into two sources. The phrase העם קראתי in vs. 24 has always been enigmatic and is often emended, but in any case, it need not indicate the total public as opposed to the thirty

guests. As for the notion of specially prepared meat for Saul, the citations made by Seebass merely indicate that meat was 'put aside' (שׂים אֹתֹ עִמָּךְ) and 'kept' (שׁמוּר) for him. If Saul arrived last of the guests, any meat set aside would naturally also be the 'remainder' (הנשׁאר).

[60]N. Habel, "The Form and Significance of the Call Narratives," *ZAW*, 77 (1965), pp. 297-323.

[61]*Ibid.*, p. 298.

[62]*Ibid.*, p. 299.

[63]We are reading with the Septuagint. The Masoretic Text omits עֹני.

[64]Both here and in subsequent discussion we are, with most scholars, reading the longer LXX version in 10:1. The verse would then read in Hebrew something such as: הלוא משׁחך יהוה לנגיד על-עמו על-ישׂראל ואתה תעצר בעם יהוה ואתה תושׁיענו מיד איביו מסביב וזה לך האות כי-משׁחך יהוה על-נחלתו לנגיד. S. R. Driver, *Notes on the Hebrew Text and the Topography of the Books of Samuel*, 2nd edition, (Oxford: Clarendon Press, 1913), p. 78, points out that the omission in MT is easily explained by "the supposition that a transcriber's eye passed from the first משׁחך יהוה to the second."

[65]Habel, *op. cit.*, p. 299.

[66]This difference in the content of the commission has led Richter, *Traditionsgeschichtliche Untersuchungen zum Richterbuch*, pp. 149-55, to delineate two types of call schemas, one for the deliverer who is called to save Israel and one for the prophet who is to proclaim God's word. The call of the deliverer is also said to lack a vision. It would, however, seem unnecessary to posit two different schemas. Even for Richter, the relationship of the two is close, and differences in content within a form do not require the positing of a second form. It would seem more likely that the call shcema used to validate the authority of the prophets as God's messengers (see Habel) was given wider application possibly in traditions whose preservation may be traced to prophetic circles. Certainly in the case of Gideon and Saul, it is easy to see prophetic circles as interested in the preservation of northern, tribal league traditions and hence, influencing the form of the tradition. In Saul's case, the purpose is also to show the role Samuel (here seen as prophet) played in anointing the man who is to become king.

[67]The origin and meaning of anointing in Israel has been the subject of considerable discussion. Although the idea that the king was divinely installed was common in the ancient Near East, anointing is not widely attested. Hittite kings were anointed by the people on accession to the throne, and in Egypt is found the practice of anointing high officials and vassal kings. There is no evidence that the Pharaoh was anointed. Scholars are divided on the influence either of these had on

Israel's practice. M. Noth, "Office and Vocation in the Old Testament," *The Laws in the Pentateuch and Other Studies*, p. 239, believes anointing came into Israel from the Hittite practice mediated by Canaanite custom. R. de Vaux, "Le roi d'Israel, vassal de Yahvé," *Mélanges Eugène Tisserant*, vol. I (Rome, 1964), pp. 119ff., argues that Israel was influenced by anointing as a rite of vassalage to Egypt, and adopted anointing for her kings because she viewed the king as the vassal of Yahweh. R. Clements, *Abraham and David: Gen. 15 and its Meaning for Israelite Tradition*, (Naperville: Alec Allenson, 1967), p. 49, agrees that anointing was adopted from acquaintance with Egyptian practice and that its interpretation as a sign of vassalage to Yahweh does appear. However, he feels it is improbable that this interpretation explains the borrowing of the custom. "At first it must have been a purely historical borrowing of a ceremonial rite, to which more than one interpretation could be attached." E. Kutsch, *Salbung als Rechtsakt im Alten Testament und im alten Orient*, *BZAW*, 88 (Berlin: Alfred Töpelmann, 1963), in an extremely helpful study, has made an important distinction between those passages that speak of anointing by the people and those that make God, acting through a prophet, the subject of the act. The former (II Sam. 2:4; 5:3; II Kgs. 11:12; 23:30) more accurately reflects the origins of the ceremony in Israel, and the latter (I Sam. 9:16; 10:1; 15:1, 17; 16:12f.; II Sam. 12:7; II Kgs. 9:3, 6, 12; II Chron. 22:7) represents a later development in the Judean king ritual to show God as the source of the authority and power bestowed in the anointing. Kutsch does fail to see that anointment by the people does not necessarily preclude the view that they were acting as Yahweh's agents and the king could still be called Yahweh's anointed. The fact that both types of anointing exist for David (II Sam. 2:4; 5:3 and I Sam. 16:12f.) tends to support Kutsch. If the LXX is read in I Sam. 11:15, we may even have evidence for an anointment of Saul where Samuel acts as the agent of the people in contrast to I Sam. 9:16; 10:1. This would tie in with the request of the elders in I Sam. 8. Rolf Knierim, "The Messianic Concept in the First Book of Samuel," *Jesus and the Historian*, edited by F. Thomas Trotter, agrees that anointment by the people was the original practice. He then suggests that the anointment of Saul in 10:1 represents a prophetic reinterpretation to emphasize the subsequent view that anointing was from Yahweh through his prophets. In its form here it represents the northern view, preserved in prophetic circles in the south after the fall of Samaria, that this anointing resulted in the bestowal of charisma. In contrast, anointing as a part of the Judean king ritual led directly to enthronement. "According to I Sam. 10:6-13 and 16:13b, the anointing belongs neither to the enthronement nor to the public act of power. Its immediate consequence is the possession of the Spirit. The first concern of this stratum is, therefore, to show that the anointing brings about the transference of the Spirit of Yahweh. This leads to two conclusions. (1) The picture of the bearer of power and of the king is that of the authorized bearer of the Spirit... (2) The receiving of the Spirit, the display of power, and the enthronement are a consequence of the anointing" (p. 31). In conclusion, we might speculate that the change in interpretation from anointing by

the people to anointing by Yahweh corresponds to increased influence of the Egyptian type of anointing. This would lend
some support to de Vaux's thesis of a vassal motif in order to
emphasize Yahweh as the true sovereign.

[68]The relationship of the term נגיד to kingship is problematic. A. Alt, "The Formation of the Israelite State in Palestine," *Essays on Old Testament History and Religion*, (Oxford:
Basil Blackwell, 1966), p. 195, suggests it is the title for
the king-designate. M. Noth, *The History of Israel*, (New York:
Harper and Bros., 1960), p. 169, agrees but suggests that נגיד
originally carried a military connotation. Both views would
accord well with the use of the term in 9:16 and 10:1. However, it was W. Richter, "Die nagid-Formel," *BZ*, 9 (1965), 71-
84, who first noticed that the title does not appear in isola-
tion but in a similarly recurring phrase. In a careful study
of this formula, Richter concludes that its consistency indicates that it existed prior to its contexts and notes that
anointing cannot be considered to have an original connection
to the title since it appears in connection with the formula
only in I Sam. 9:16 and 10:1. He does trace the formula to
northern origins and feels it was later connected with kingship
in the developing theology of the Davidic monarchy. I Kgs. 1:
35 states that David made Solomon נגיד over Israel *and* Judah
which shows that the title was not an all-Israel title but belonged to the north and was appropriated by the south. The
northern origin of the title may have commended it to a prophetic editor for use in 9:16 and 10:1 since Saul was not yet
king, but he wished to indicate that this was Saul's ultimate
destiny growing out of his anointing.

[69]Habel, *op. cit.*, p. 301.

[70]This explains why the fulfillment of 10:2-4 is not narrated. These predictions were not considered signs in the call
schema as was the encounter with the prophets. It should also
be mentioned that vs. 9 refers to "signs" and this is probably
to be considered the original conclusion to the predictions of
Samuel in the folk tale tradition. Here as in 10:6 Saul is to
be a changed man, but in conflict with 10:6, the change is before the signs take place. Hence, 10:9 should be placed with
10:2-4 and cannot belong with 10:5-8.

[71]To be sure, the origins of I Sam. 11 are quite apart
from those of 10:5-8, but we feel they have been linked pur-
posefully in the editorial shaping and ordering of the Saul
material. Thus, chapter 11 now serves as the public functioning of the charisma which validates the call of Saul through
the anointing and the possession by the spirit. For the reader
who knows the story of Saul, 10:5-8 becomes a capsule history
of his career as God's anointed.

[72]D. R. Ap-Thomas, "Saul's Uncle," *VT*, 11 (1961), pp. 241-
45, interprets the figure of the uncle as a Philistine official
from whom Saul is hiding his military mission. The view rests,
however, on unsound philological evidence and has received
little support.

[73]Smith, *Books of Samuel*, *ICC*, pp. xviiff.; Driver, *Introduction*, pp. 175ff.; Pfeiffer, *Introduction*, pp. 359f.; Muilenburg, *Tell En-Nasbeh*, pp. 23ff.; Caird, *I and II Samuel*, *IB*, vol. 2, pp. 935ff.

[74]Noth, *Überlieferungsgeschichtliche Studien*, pp. 54-60. Wellhausen, *Prolegomena*, pp. 245-72, while assigning this to the late source saw some Deuteronomic connections as did Kennedy, *Samuel*, pp. 14ff. Schunck, *Benjamin*, pp. 80ff., agrees with Noth that the section is an old tradition reworked by the Deuteronomist.

[75]O. Eissfeldt, *Die Komposition der Samuelisbücher*, (Leipzig: J. C. Hinrichs, 1931), p. 7. He assigns 10:17-21bα to his E source and 10:21bβ-27 to his L source. G. Fohrer, "Der Vertrag zwischen König und Volk in Israel," *ZAW*, 71 (1959), pp. 1-22, concurs with Eissfeldt that there is an old tradition fragment in 10:21bβ-27. Seebass, "Traditionsgeschichte von I Sam. 8, 10:17ff., und 12," *ZAW*, 77 (1965), pp. 286ff., argues against a division at 21bβ but posits instead two versions of the lottery, one involving the Matrite family of which no one is believed present and another involving Saul who is hidden. Such a view receives no literary support in the text, and Seebass fails to give any convincing evidence for his theory. His division shows that he has failed to understand the nature of the lot-casting process as will be seen below.

[76]Driver, *Notes on the Hebrew Text and the Topography of the Books of Samuel*, p. 85.

[77]Eissfeldt, *op. cit.*, p. 7.

[78]Eissfeldt sees this tradition fragment as including all of 10:21bβ-27, but as we shall see at a later point, there is ample reason to believe that it ends with vs. 24.

[79]Seebass, *op. cit.*

[80]J. Lindblom, "Lot-casting in the Old Testament," *VT*, 12 (1962), pp. 164-78.

[81]We shall leave the question of the relationship between vss. 20-21bα and vss. 17-19 until after our discussion of 17-19.

[82]Noth, *op. cit.*, p. 58, n. 2.

[83]C. J. Labuschagne, *The Incomparability of Yahweh in the Old Testament*, (Leiden: E. J. Brill, 1966), pp. 9-10.

[84]*Ibid.*, p. 10.

[85]W. Richter, *Die Bearbeitungen des "Retterbuches" in der deuteronomischen Epoche*, p. 106.

[86]*Ibid.*, pp. 105-06.

[87]Richter characterizes these as *Botenformel*, *Herausführungsformel* and *Rettungsformel*. It should also be noted here that there is one element which appears in Richter's list of Dtr elements and in I Sam. 10:17ff. It is the use in both of the etymologically related verbs צעק/זעק. This similarity dissolves, however, on closer examination since זעק in Jdgs. 6 refers to a cry for help whereas צעק in I Sam. 10:17 is merely a call to assembly.

[88]C. Westermann, *Basic Forms of Prophetic Speech*, (Philadelphia: Westminster Press, 1967), pp. 98ff.

[89]*Ibid.*, pp. 182-83.

[90]W. H. Schmidt, "Die deuteronomistische Redaktion des Amosbuches," *ZAW*, 77 (1965), pp. 168-93. It should be noted that Schmidt's argument that Amos 2:9-12 is Deuteronomistic rests on matters of vocabulary and theme rather than formal considerations.

[91]Westermann, *op. cit.*, p. 183.

[92]*Ibid.*, pp. 186-87.

[93]Wellhausen, *Prolegomena*, pp. 245-72.

[94]Karl Budde, *Die Bücher Samuel* (Tübingen: J.C.B. Mohr, 1902).

[95]Driver, *Introduction*, p. 175; Kennedy, *Samuel*, pp. 14ff.; Pfeiffer, *Introduction*, pp. 344ff.; Caird, *I and II Samuel*, IB, p. 857; Noth, *Überlieferungsgeschichtliche Studien*, pp. 57ff. Driver and Noth both see only vs. 14 as representing the influence of later redactors. Noth identifies the hand responsible for vs. 14 as the Deuteronomistic historian that he believes is responsible for the present order of material in I Samuel.

[96]Lods, *Israel*, p. 354; Eissfeldt, *Komposition*. The latter places the chapter in his L source except for 6a which is J.

[97]Weiser, *Samuel*, pp. 69ff.; Hertzberg, *I and II Samuel*, pp. 91ff.; Schunck, *Benjamin*, pp. 107ff.

[98]Alt, *Essays*, pp. 185-86; Wildberger, "Samuel und die Entstehung des israelitischen Königtums," *Theologische Zeitschrift*, 13 (1957), pp. 442ff.; Irwin, "Samuel and the Rise of the Monarchy," *AJSL*, 58 (1941), pp. 113ff.

[99]M. Tsevat, "The Biblical Narrative of the Foundation of Kingship in Israel," (Hebr.), *Tarbiz*, 36 (1966), pp. 99-109, has recently argued that 11:12-15 serves as an introduction to chapter 12. While it is true that the assembly at Gilgal may have provided the occasion for attaching the speech of Samuel in chapter 12, the materials themselves are so different in form and content as to provide no basis for arguing an original connection.

[100] However, Saul's blowing of the horn in 13:3 may also relate to the muster of the tribal levy.

[101] Richter, *Traditionsgeschichtliche Untersuchungen*, pp. 177ff.

[102] See above, pp. 17-18.

[103] Richter, *op. cit.*, pp. 177ff.

[104] Originally the mission of the messengers was a desperation move by the men of Jabesh-Gilead which was miraculously answered by Saul's rescue, but the search for a deliverer takes on new meaning when 11:1ff. is incorporated into the order of traditions as we now have them in I Samuel. Now in light of the previous traditions, the reader knows that a potential deliverer is at hand and it is to be expected that he will respond. Indeed, as we shall see, his response and victory are the vindication of his election.

[105] The RSV translation misses this double meaning entirely by translating "Tomorrow we will give ourselves up to you." The phrase מחר נצא אליכם would be better translated as "Tomorrow we will come out to you." Naturally the Ammonites would take this as an acceptance of surrender terms, but the reader now knows that it means a coming battle.

[106] M. Buber, *Kingship of God*, (New York: Harper and Row, 1967), p. 79, has suggested that Jdgs. 19-21 has been consciously composed with numerous similarities to I Sam. 11 in an attempt by anti-Benjaminite (or anti-Saul) factions to counteract the positive picture of I Sam. 11. Although suggestive, this hypothesis would require a careful study of Jdgs. 19-21 which lies beyond the scope of this study.

[107] Eissfeldt, *Komposition*, p. 63.

[108] Against Seebass, *ZAW*, 79 (1967), p. 155ff., who believes the Ammonite victory led only to Saul's *nagid*-ship. However, he supports this only by arguing that the present text is confused, and he then proceeds to an extensive rearrangement of material with very little support in the text itself. He has assumed a certain historical course of events and then rearranged his texts. There is no convincing literary reason for believing that the account of Saul's accession to the throne in 11:15 does not belong with I Sam. 11:1-11.

[109] R. Knierim, "The Messianic Concept in the First Book of Samuel," *Jesus and the Historian*, edited by F. Thomas Trotter, pp. 28ff.

[110] Significantly this anointment, as with Saul, is followed by a possession by the spirit.

[111] Merrill, *I Sam. 1-12*, pp. 172-79.

[112]*Ibid.* Merrill feels that 10:27a and 11:12-13 are unrelated since the former asks whether Saul can save them while the latter questions his right to be king. The point is lost, however, when vs. 15 makes clear that even at the earliest level of the tradition Saul's ability to deliver the people is closely related to the authority of his kingship. The notice of vss. 12-13 makes this point itself when Saul's response (vs. 13) is in terms of the deliverance that has been accomplished. The focus is on the sacral/legal violations of those who have slandered God's anointed.

[113]The question of Saul's opponents is incomplete in the MT (שאול ימלך עלינו). Either an interrogative ה should be supplied or the negative particle לא should be read following the LXX.

[114]Knierim, *op. cit.*, p. 33.

[115]Gerhard von Rad, *Old Testament Theology*, 2 vols. (New York: Harper and Bros., 1962, 1965), I, pp. 326ff.

[116]Wellhausen, *Prolegomena*, pp. 245-72; Smith, *Books of Samuel*, ICC, pp. xviff.; Pfeiffer, *Introduction*, pp. 359ff.; Driver, *Introduction*, pp. 175f.; Caird, *I and II Samuel*, IB, pp. 941ff.; Eissfeldt, *Komposition*, places I Sam. 12 in his E source.

[117]Noth, *Überlieferungsgeschichtliche Studien*, pp. 5, 59-60.

[118]*Ibid.*, p. 5.

[119]Dennis McCarthy, "II Samuel 7 and the Structure of the Deuteronomic History," *JBL*, 84 (1965), pp. 131ff., adds II Sam. 7 to the list of key interpretive passages placed as speeches in the mouths of key figures by the Deuteronomist.

[120]Weiser, *Samuel*, pp. 79ff.; Hertzberg, *I and II Samuel*.

[121]Seebass, "Traditionsgeschichte von I Sam. 8, 10:17ff. und 12," *ZAW*, 77 (1965), pp. 286ff. He limits the old tradition to 12:1-6a, 7a, 6b, 13b, 14b, 24b, 25 and finds Deuteronomic influence in 12:7b-12aα, 14a, 15-24a.

[122]M. Buber, "Die Erzählung von Sauls Königswahl," *Vetus Testamentum*, 6 (1956), pp. 113ff.

[123]Dennis McCarthy, *Treaty and Covenant* (Rone: Pontifical Biblical Institute, 1963), p. 141.

[124]It should be noted, however, that neither kingship nor Saul as such is condemned. The focus is on the rebellious will of the people.

[125]K. Galling, "Der Beichtspiegel: eine gattungsgeschichtliche Studie," *ZAW*, 47 (1929), pp. 125-30, first identified this formal type, but it was G. von Rad, "The Early History of

the Form-Category of I Cor. 13:4-7," *The Problem of the Hexateuch and Other Essays*, (New York: McGraw-Hill, 1966), pp. 301ff., who first noticed that I Sam. 12:3-4 was related to it.

[126] G. von Rad, *op. cit.*, p. 314.

[127] Our discussion at this point owes much to James Muilenburg, "The Form and Structure of the Covenantal Formulations," , 9 (1959), pp. 347-65; and McCarthy, *Treaty and Covenant*, pp. 141ff.

[128] McCarthy, *op. cit.*

[129] *Ibid.*, p. 142.

[130] *Ibid.* McCarthy reports the suggestion of Lohfink in *Scholastik*, 36 (1961), pp. 423f., that "13b ist zwecks Erzeugung eines Chiasmus vorangezogene Apodosis des Segens," but objects that "the blessing and curse are usually constructed as parallels, which would mean that the threat in 15 should be loss of the king. Besides, could 13b, connected with the foregoing by *waw*, actually belong to what follows?"

[131] McCarthy, *op. cit.*, p. 143.

[132] Seebass, *op. cit.*, pp. 288ff.

[133] See note 27.

[134] McCarthy, *Treaty and Covenant*, pp. 138-39, 144.

[135] McCarthy, *JBL*, 84 (1965), p. 136.

[136] Wellhausen, *Prolegomena*, p. 257; Driver, *Introduction*, p. 175ff.; Pfeiffer, *Introduction*, pp. 342ff.; Irwin, *AJSL*, 58 (1941), pp. 113ff.; Buber, *VT*, 6 (1956), pp. 113ff.; Wildberger, *ThZ*, 13 (1957), pp. 442ff.; Hertzberg, *I and II Samuel*, pp. 103ff.

[137] Eissfeldt, *Komposition*, divides as follows: 13:1, 3abβ, 4a, 6, 7a, 16-21 (22) - L; 13:3bα, 4b-5, 7b-15a, (15b) - J. Horst Seebass, "I Sam. 15 als Schlüssel für das Verständnis der sogenannten königsfreundlichen Reihe I Sam. 9:1-10:16, 11:1-15; und 13:2-14:52," *ZAW*, 79 (1967), pp. 149ff., divides the chapter into two old sources: A. 13:2, 3a, 3bβ, 6, 7a, 19-22; B. 13:4, 3bα, 5, 7b-18, 23. F. Mildenberger, *Die vordeuteronomistische Saul-David-Überlieferung*, Diss. Tübingen, 1962, separates 13:4b, 5, 7b-15a from the rest of the chapter.

[138] Schunck, *Benjamin*, pp. 107-08.

[139] Seebass, *op. cit.*

[140] It should be mentioned that most scholars attribute the chronological note of 13:1 to the Deuteronomistic writer although they do not find his influence elsewhere in the chapter.

[141] Noth, *Überlieferungsgeschichtliche Studien*, p. 63.

[142]Virtually all commentators have observed that the place names Gibeah (גבעה) and Geba (גבע) have often been confused in the Old Testament. The Masoretic Text in vs. 16 reads גבע בנימן but we contend that this should be read גבעה בנימן in light of the references in 13:15a (LXX) and 14:2. Geba appears elsewhere with the attached tribal name only in I Kgs. 15:22. An apparent occurrence in Jdgs. 20:10 must be read Gibeah due to the overwhelming evidence in Jdgs. 19-20 of nineteen references to Gibeah as the location for the event reported there. A similar confusion has occurred in I Sam. 13:16.

[143]R. J. Williams, *Hebrew Syntax: An Outline* (Toronto: University of Toronto Press, 1968), pp. 32, 42, 96.

[144]Wellhausen, *Prolegomena*, p. 257, advanced a similar argument for the secondary character of vss. 7b-15a. "Vers. 16, however, gives us the impression that Saul had been posted at Gibeah with his men for some time when the Philistines took up their camp over against them. Only in this way is justice done to the contrasted participle of state (*sedentes*) and inchoative perfect (*castrametati sunt*)."

[145]We shall see below that 13:1-7a, 15b-18 belongs originally with the narrative of chapter 14.

[146]See, for example, G. B. Caird, "I and II Samuel," *IB*, vol. 2, p. 946.

[147]See, for example, H. P. Smith, *Books of Samuel*, *ICC*, p. 92. Renewed confidence in the LXX readings for Samuel may give this argument greater support.

[148]Noth, *Überlieferungsgeschichtliche Studien*, pp. 18ff.

[149]*Ibid.*; and Noth, *History of Israel*, pp. 176-77.

[150]We are, for the moment, excluding vss. 19-22 which we will discuss below.

[151]The word נציב appears only nine times in BH and has been variously translated. In Gen. 19:26, the word clearly means a pillar of some sort; in I Kgs. 4:19, the word is just as clearly intended as the name of an officer of some sort, usually rendered 'prefect,' and in II Sam. 8:6, 14, the word must be taken as 'garrison.' All three meanings have been supported for I Sam. 10:5 and 13:3 with the supporters of 'pillar' suggesting this was some sort of symbol for Philistine dominion which Jonathan struck down as an act of rebellion. This, however, seems a rather minor act to create the stir implied in succeeding verses. We would read either garrison or prefect, implying that Jonathan's act was a military encounter.

[152]Reading with LXX and the Targums.

[153]LXX and Vulgate express after מן-הגלגל a long addition which serves to get Saul back to Gibeah from Gilgal. It can be reconstructed in Hebrew somewhat as follows: וילך לדרכו ויתר

126

הָעָם עָלָה אַחֲרֵי שָׁאוּל לִקְרַאת עַם-הַמִּלְחָמָה וַיָּבֹאוּ מִן-הַגִּלְגָּל, "and went his way. And the people who were left went up after Saul to meet the men of war and they came from Gilgal (MT continues from here) to Gibeah of Benjamin." The long section probably dropped out due to the repetition of מִן-הַגִּלְגָּל.

[154]We are greatly indebted in the following discussion to Westermann, *Basic Forms of Prophetic Speech*, pp. 129ff.

[155]This is clearly related to Samuel's instructions in 10:8, but we shall reserve a discussion on the nature of this relationship until a later point.

[156]Although Saul asks for both the עֹלָה and the שְׁלָמִים, he offers only the עֹלָה. It could be that Samuel arrived before Saul could offer the שְׁלָמִים; or, as some have suggested, the שְׁלָמִים could be considered a constituent part of the עֹלָה, a hypothesis which might find support in II Sam. 24:22ff. See R. Rendtorff, *Studien zur Geschichte des Opfers im alten Israel*, (Neukirchen: Neukirchener Verlag, 1967), pp. 124ff.

[157]See R. de Vaux, *Ancient Israel*, p. 259.

[158]Westermann, *op. cit.*, p. 144.

[159]Cf. *ibid.*, p. 134, for a discussion of the prophet as the messenger of God, the judge, and his role as the watchman over God's law.

[160]*Ibid.*, p. 154.

[161]*Ibid.*, p. 148.

[162]*Ibid.*, p. 138.

[163]A. R. S. Kennedy, *Samuel*, *The Century Bible*, suggests this is late priestly propaganda showing a type of "closed shop" attitude. J. L. McKenzie, "The Four Samuels," *Biblical Research*, 7 (1962), pp. 3-18, also believes the tradition to be of priestly origin.

[164]R. Bach, *Die Aufforderungen zur Flucht und zum Kampf im alttestamentlichen Prophetenspruch*. See also R. Rendtorff, "Reflections on the Early History of Prophecy in Israel," *History and Hermeneutics*, edited by Robert Funk (New York: Harper and Row, 1967), pp. 14ff.

[165]Wellhausen, *Die Composition des Hexateuchs und der historischen Bücher des Alten Testaments*, p. 248.

[166]Budde, *Die Bücher Samuel*, p. 187; Smith, *I and II Samuel*, *ICC*, p. 120.

[167]A. Lods, *Israel from its Beginnings to the Middle of the Eighth Century*.

[168]Schunck, *Benjamin*, pp. 107-08. However, Noth, *Über-lieferungsgeschichtliche Studien*, p. 63, has stressed the fact that he can see no clues to Deuteronomistic work in the chapter.

[169]Smith, *I and II Samuel*, ICC, pp. xviff.; Driver, *Introduction*, pp. 175ff.; Pfeiffer, *Introduction*, pp. 344ff.; Kennedy, *Samuel*, *The Century Bible*, p. 16; Noth, *Überlieferungs-geschichtliche Studien*, pp. 61ff.; Hertzberg, *I and II Samuel*, pp. 111ff.; Weiser, *Introduction*, pp. 162f.; Caird, "Books of Samuel," *IB*, p. 857.

[170]Eissfeldt, *Komposition*, p. 11.

[171]H. Seebass, "I Sam. 15 als Schlüssel für das Verständnis der sogenannten königsfreundlichen Reihe I Sam. 9:1-10:16, 11:1-15; und 13:2-14:52," *ZAW*, 79 (1967), pp. 149ff.

[172]See n. 169.

[173]Schunck, *Benjamin*, pp. 107-08, feels the summaries are insertions from Jerusalem archival material. Weiser, *Introduction*, pp. 162-63, sees these verses as the concluding summaries of a loose collection of material on the rise of Saul (9:1-10:16; 11; 13; 14). Noth, *Überlieferungsgeschichtliche Studien*, p. 63, states only that he believes the verses are secondary but stresses that there is no reason to consider them as Deuteronomistic.

[174]J. Blenkinsopp, "Jonathan's Sacrilege," *CBQ*, 26 (1964), p. 424, although defending the unity of chapter 14, discusses some of these difficulties.

[175]Vs. 28b is often emended as a pointless anticipation of vs. 31b, but this is not necessary and in fact leaves us unclear as to the relationship of the people's behaviour in vss. 31-35 to Saul's imposed fast in vs. 24.

[176]Richter, *Traditionsgeschichtliche Untersuchungen zum Richterbuch*, p. 263.

[177]J. Blenkinsopp, *op. cit.*, has done a thorough analysis of I Sam. 14:1-46 in terms of literary style. Although we cannot feel as confident in matters of rhythm and assonance as he does, the article makes many interesting observations.

[178]See G. von Rad, *Der Heilige Krieg im alten Israel* (Zürich: Zwingli, 1951), pp. 6ff.; Richter, *Traditionsgeschichtliche Untersuchungen zum Richterbuch*, pp. 52-53; R. de Vaux, *Ancient Israel*, pp. 259ff.

[179]See Richter, *op. cit.*, pp. 21ff., for a detailed discussion of this formula.

[180]Gressmann, *Die Schriften des Alten Testaments*, part 2, vol. 1, pp. 52f.

[181]Hertzberg, *I and II Samuel*, p. 119.

[182]See the discussion in Driver, *Notes on the Hebrew Text of Samuel*, p. 120.

[183]Budde, *Die Bücher Samuel*; Smith, *I and II Samuel*, *ICC*, pp. xviff.; Alt, "Formation of the Israelite State in Palestine," *Essays*, pp. 185-86; Eissfeldt, *Komposition*, placed chapter 15 in his E source.

[184]Pfeiffer, *Introduction*, p. 367. Schunck, *Benjamin*, pp. 107-08, sees in vss. 4a, 5, 8a and 12b a nucleus of old tradition which has been reworked by the Deuteronomist.

[185]Seebass, *ZAW*, 79 (1967), pp. 155ff. His division leaves vss. 15, 20a, 21-22, 30b, 31b, and 35b unaccounted for. In any case, such an extensive division can only be supported on the basis of preconceived notions of the historical course of events and has little support in the text itself.

[186]Noth, *Überlieferungsgeschichtliche Studien*, p. 63.

[187]P. Mildenberger, *Die vordeuteronomistische Saul-David-Überlieferung* (Diss., Tübingen, 1962).

[188]Hertzberg, *I and II Samuel*, pp. 123f. We shall examine his hypothesis more closely at a later point.

[189]Driver, *Introduction*, p. 178.

[190]A. Weiser, "I Samuel 15," *ZAW*, 54 (1936), pp. 1ff.

[191]See note 185 above.

[192]Pfeiffer, *op. cit.*; Noth, *op. cit.*

[193]G. von Rad, *Der Heilige Krieg im alten Israel*.

[194]As in our discussion of 13:7b-15a, we are indebted to Westermann, *Basic Forms of Prophetic Speech*, for his excellent discussion of prophetic speech forms.

[195]Westermann, *Basic Forms of Prophetic Speech*, p. 142.

[196]*Ibid.*, p. 134. "God, then, watches over the law and he can demand that the king stand before judgment. It is God, therefore, who hands down the decision about the accused. The prophet has to transmit this decision of God to the accused; he is the messenger who brings the decision that was handed down by God before the accused--in this case the king--and proclaims it to him."

[197]It is undoubtedly somewhat artificial to divide chapter 15 into the parts of the prophetic judgment speech to an individual since the speech form itself has been thoroughly absorbed into the narrative. However, as we shall see, the various elements of the speech form can still be clearly detected, and it is our contention that vss. 14-21 are under the influence

of the accusation while vss. 26-31 are influenced by the announcement. The oracle in vss. 22-23 is a complete judgment in itself containing both accusation and announcement, and it serves to divide the narrative into the two parts mentioned above.

[198]See p. 81.

[199]Westermann, *op. cit.*, p. 157. He also cites a parallel to this contrast motif in the Mari letters to show that it was not a later development in the form.

[200]*Ibid.*, p. 148.

[201]*Ibid.*, pp. 160-61.

[202]R. Knierim, *Die Hauptbegriffe für Sünde im Alten Testament* (Gütersloh: Gütersloher Verlagshaus Gerd Mohn, 1965), pp. 20ff.

[203]Westermann, *op. cit.*, pp. 158-59.

[204]Cf. p. 83.

[205]See, for example, McKenzie, "The Four Samuels," *BR*, 7 (1962), pp. 3-18, where he attributes 13:7b-15a to priestly circles and chapter 15 to prophetic circles.

[206]Knierim, "The Messianic Concept in the First Book of Samuel," *Jesus and the Historian*, edited by F. Thomas Trotter, p. 38.

[207]A. Weiser, "I Samuel 15," *ZAW*, 54 (1936), pp. 2f.

[208]Hertzberg, *I and II Samuel*, pp. 123-24.

CHAPTER III

THE GROWTH AND DEVELOPMENT OF I SAM. 7-15

Now that we have carefully examined the character of the
tradition materials which make up chapters 7-15, we must attempt to draw our analysis of this material into a coherent
picture of the process through which these chapters came into
their present shape. We shall argue that the beginning and the
end of this process are easily distinguished. The beginning is
a sizable group of old and independent traditions, some still
essentially complete and some discernible only as fragments.
At the end of the process stands the work of the Deuteronomist.
His influence is clearly discernible at certain points, but we
shall argue that it is not as extensive as often claimed. Having thus separated these two stages at the opposite ends of the
development of chapters 7-15, we will turn to the central question of the editorial work which intervened. Here we will attempt to show that an editor prior to the Deuteronomist has
gathered and ordered the material concerning Saul's rise to the
kingship and his subsequent rejection. He has used old tradition material but has also contributed material that bears his
own peculiar stamp. Our hypothesis is that this edition finds
its provenance in early prophetic circles whose nature and interests we will attempt to delineate. Our final conclusion is
that the Deuteronomist found himself basically sympathetic to
the prophetic edition he found before him; thus, his own work
in this material is essentially supplementary and not at all
extensive.

I

The analysis of chapters 7-15 discloses that at the earliest distinguishable level lies a sizable group of old, independent traditions, concerning the period of the establishment
of the kingship in Israel. A list of the main passages in
which these old traditions may be detected will indicate their
extent and variety.[1]

7:7-12	Victory over the Philistines, aetiology of Ebenezer.
15-17	Samuel's judicial circuit.
8:1-7	The corruption of Samuel's sons and the people's request for a king.
9:1-14, 18-19, 22-24; 10:2-4, 9, 14-16a	Folk tale of Saul's search for the lost asses.
10:10-12	Aetiology of the proverb, "Is Saul also among the prophets?"
20-24	Saul's choice by lot and/or because of his stature.
26-27	Opposition to Saul.
11:1-11	Saul's victory over the Ammonites.
15	Saul's elevation to the kingship.
(13-14)	Collection of materials centering on Saul's military exploits.
13:2-7a, 15b-23	Archival material on military movements during the Philistine war.
14:1-46	Narrative account of Jonathan's surprise attack and sacrilege.
47-52	Concluding summary and genealogy.

A glance at this list quickly shows that it in no way resembles the usual division into pericopes from which most studies of chapters 7-15 begin (7; 8; 9:1-10:16; 10:17-27; 11; 12; 13-14; 15). For the most part, these customary divisions have been made on the basis of subject matter and not critical analysis. The usual pericopes certainly cannot be used as the basic units of tradition in the discussion of these chapters.

The list of the old tradition material contains a wide variety of types of material. Among these might be mentioned aetiological narratives (7:7-12; 10:10-12), a folkloristic narrative (9:1-14, 18-19, 22-24; 10:2-4, 9, 14-16a), archival material (14:47-51), a historical note (13:19-22), and narratives of military encounters (11:1-11; 14:1ff.). As well as showing a great diversity in types of material, these old traditions also display a wide variety in their state of preservation. Some are presently found in chapters 7-15 as essentially complete traditions. A good example might be the account of Saul's Ammonite victory in 11:1-11. On the other hand, there are clearly old traditions which are now preserved for the reader only in fragmentary form, and these fragments are now found in an entirely different context. This may be seen in 10:20-24 where fragments of two old traditions (one on Saul's choice by lot; the other on his designation because of his height) are found in an entirely different setting. It is not clear whether the two fragments were combined by the later editor who placed them here or had already been joined at an earlier stage. Still other old traditions, while still detectable, have been subjected to a rather thorough reworking in connection with later editorial activity. The folk tale of Saul's search for the lost asses (9:1-14, 18-19, 22-24; 10:2-4, 9, 14-16a) has been used as the occasion for, and been blended into, obviously later material of quite a different character. In chapter 8, what is obviously old material concerning the failure of Samuel's sons and the people's request for a king sets forth what we have called a "sinful-but-still-of-God" view of kingship. This material has been supplemented and reinterpreted by a later Deuteronomistic addition. For the most part, these old traditions seem isolated from one another, but one small collection of material can be found in 13:2-7a, 15b-23; 14:1-52. Although there are several different types of material within this complex, the analysis shows clear connections between the material of chapter 13 and that of 14. The concluding summary and genealogy were attributed to the small collection because they made little sense and were completely out of place as the concluding notes for a later and larger edition. This small collection centered on Saul's military matters (mostly Philistine) and is the only example detected of a tendency of the old traditions to come together into source documents which were employed by later editors. Aside from this minor example, no evidence of sources could be found. As for date, apart from stating that there is no reason to date any of these traditions at a great distance from the time of Saul, little more can be said. The matter of an exact date would have to be taken up independently for each separate tradition, and this lies beyond the scope or purpose of this study.

With such a wide diversity of traditions generalization is risky at best, but perhaps a few cautious remarks might be

made. It should be pointed out that in the old traditions
there are two versions of Saul's elevation to the kingship:[2]
in the one, he was chosen by lot and/or indicated by his height
at an assembly of the people (10:20-24), while in the second
he was made king following his victory over the Ammonites (11:
15). As we have seen, a later hand has harmonized these two
with the addition of 11:14. In general, it might also be said
that the attitude toward Saul in the old traditions is a positive one although it is made clear that Saul was not without
some opposition (10:26-27). It may be that the reluctance of
Samuel in chapter 8 is firmly based on an old tradition recording some resistance to the idea of a king, especially among
those who might be said to represent the old tribal league.
Samuel's role in the old traditions is worthy of note. In the
first instance he appears much less frequently in these materials than he does in the chapters as they now stand. Further,
in 7:15-17, we have one of the few sections concerning Samuel
that scholars generally agree is old and genuine. It tells us
that Samuel regularly traveled a circuit composed of some of
the chief cultic centers in Israel, and that there he judged
Israel. Samuel can, thus, be described as a judge in this instance (not in the sense of the charismatic heroes of the Book
of Judges, but as a magistrate). Samuel is also apparently a
judge in chapter 8 when the people approach him concerning the
breakdown in the administration of justice.[3] The nature of
office in the period of the league cannot be pursued here.
Noth has plausibly suggested the existence of an office of
"judge of Israel" and has suggested that Samuel was a holder
of this office.[4] This would make him, in the oldest traditions, an official of the league in a period when there was no
central sanctuary, and this might explain his travel to various
cult centers. Weiser's warning that one must not make too
sharp a division between the offices of judge and cultic officer in this period is well taken.[5] The league itself was cul-
tically oriented, and any of its officials might be assumed to
have certain connections to the cultus. This might well explain the notice of Samuel's building of an altar in 7:17 or
his sacrificial role in 7:7ff. In any case, we are forced to

admit that almost nothing is known of how such hypothetical
league officials were appointed or of what the full range of
their duties might have been. We can only state that the oldest traditions picture Samuel as a judge (magistrate) and probably in this capacity as an official of the tribal league.
Another picture of Samuel emerges in the folk tale of 9:1-14,
18-19, 22-24; 10:2-4, 9, 14-16a. Here Samuel is called a <u>seer</u>
(ראה) and a man of God (איש-אלהים). It is apparent from the
analysis of chapter 9, however, that this entire tradition is
influenced by folkloristic tendencies and cannot be used as a
basis for attempting to determine Samuel's role in the oldest
level of the tradition. Part of the nature of the tale is the
element of surprise when the listener discovers the seer to be
Samuel, and the fact that Samuel was not known as a seer may
have contributed to this unexpected denouement.

II

At the other end of the process through which chapters 7-
15 came into their present shape stands the work of the Deuteronomist.[6] In the analysis of individual passages we have identified aspects of form, vocabulary and content which serve as
the basis for identifying a passage as Deuteronomistic. Those
passages which show the clear influence of a Deuteronomistic
editor are as follows:

>   7:3-4, 13-14
>   8:8, 10-22
>   12:6-24
>   13:1

This list might be considered remarkable by some because it is
not very extensive. Especially noteworthy is the absence of
10:17ff., a passage often claimed to show Deuteronomistic influence. As we have seen, however, there is little basis for
such a claim. The reference to God's saving act in the delivery from Egypt (10:18) is contrasted to the people's present
rejection of God whereas the historical retrospect in 8:8 and
12:8ff. (clearly Deuteronomistic) serves to emphasize the theme
of continual apostasy by Israel. Further, the passage in

10:17ff. goes on to a conclusion that must be considered extremely positive to Saul's kingship, while the Deuteronomist, as we shall see, takes at best a dim view of the kingship. Our analysis finds little reason for extending the limits of Deuteronomistic influence in chapters 7-15 any further than the above list.

The methods of the Deuteronomist in this material can be briefly described. For some reason, he has certainly found it unnecessary or impossible to place his source material into a large organizing framework similar to those found in the Books of Judges or Kings. His work in chapters 7-15 seems to be more supplementary in nature. In chapter 7 he has added an introductory notice in vss. 3-4 and a concluding notice in vss. 13-14, the purpose of which seems to be to depict the victory over the Philistines as one of the deliverances which follow repentance from apostasy characteristic of the Deuteronomistic view of the period of the tribal league. In chapter 12 he has inserted one of his programmatic speeches which mark the turning points of the Deuteronomistic history work. This speech marks the turning from the period of the league to that of the kingship and combines a survey over Israel's previous sin with an admonition to obedience in covenantal terms. In 13:1 the Deuteronomist has simply placed his usual chronological formula in its proper place at the beginning of Saul's reign. Chapter 8 also shows the influence of the Deuteronomist. It is clear that he has added to an old tradition recording the people's request for a king in such a way that the request is interpreted as running the risk of the sin of apostasy. Deuteronomistic influence is obvious in vss. 8 and 18 and is probably also to be seen in the use of the phrase כל־הגוים. It may also be the Deuteronomist who is responsible for the insertion of the description of the practices of the foreign kings in vss. 11-17. It is clear that the "sinful-but-still-of-God" view of kingship was already a part of the old tradition and has been altered by the Deuteronomist in accordance with his view of the kingship.

The general concerns and emphases of the Deuteronomistic material in chapters 7-15 are in keeping with characteristics noted in standard works on the Deuteronomistic work.[7] The view of the kingship is expressed in the "law of the king" in Deut. 17:14ff. Von Rad writes concerning this law, "Kingship is conceived, almost reluctantly, as a concession to historical reality... Deuteronomy is concerned only to prevent kingship from disturbing the organization of the people's life as set forth in Deuteronomy."[8] More specifically, Deut. 17:14ff. is concerned that if Israel is to have a king he not be a foreigner or adopt foreign ways. The Deuteronomistic materials in I Sam. 8 and 12 display a similar viewpoint. The Deuteronomist is forced to come to grips with the fact that God allowed Israel to have a king, but it is clear that he is less than enthusiastic about this development. His main concern, however, is to fit the kingship into the larger framework of covenant obedience, a significant feature of his theology. The kingship is not in itself a sin, but it contains a potential for sin. This potential is spelled out in chapter 8 where the Deuteronomist goes beyond the "sinful-but-still-of-God" view in the old tradition to add his concern over the danger that the king will adopt foreign ways, thus leading to apostasy and the worship of foreign gods (8:8). This is similar to the concern in Deut. 17:14ff. Still, it is God who allows a king to be chosen (12:13), and 12:14-15 makes clear that the king as well as the people stand before the possibility of blessing or curse depending on their obedience or disobedience to God's commandment. The king, for the Deuteronomist, has no special status before God. This can be especially seen in the absence of any mention of the king as God's anointed in the clearly Deuteronomistic portions of I and II Samuel. Mention of the anointing of the king is also missing in the old traditions listed previously; hence, the setting for the motif must lie at some other point in the history of tradition. In any case, it is clear that the king is not described as God's anointed in the Deuteronomistic portions of I Sam. 7-15. The king, for the Deuteronomist, stands with all of Israel under the same demand for covenant obedience. To be sure, for Israel to have a king is an additional risk and is seen as a manifestation of Israel's tendency to turn from God into apostasy, but with all the people the king

also shares the promise of blessing if God's commandment is
obeyed. Such a view, although less than positive, is not properly characterized as anti-monarchical, since this would seem
to imply inherent evil in kingship. It might best be described
as an additional temptation, the existence of which is due to
God's tolerance.[9]

We have already touched on other interests of the Deuteronomist, and they need not be elaborated. One of these is the
interpretation of Israel's chief sin as apostasy. This is
usually expressed in terms of a turning to foreign gods and
ways, thus, a turning away from Yahweh. This concern is well-
known as a motif in the Books of Deuteronomy and Judges. This
general concern to guard against apostasy is seen in 7:3-4;
8:8; 12:8ff. An additional element in this general theme of
apostasy is the motif that Israel has *continually* sinned by
turning to foreign gods. This is seen in 8:8 and in the historical retrospect of 12:8ff. The Deuteronomist's purpose in
his additions to chapters 7-15 seems to be to interpret the
rise of kingship as another episode in this history of Israel's
tendency to apostasy and to warn against this tendency's becoming reality. Another interest in the Deuteronomist's work is
the concern for covenantal obedience already mentioned. Chapter 12 is influenced by the covenant form itself. For the Deuteronomist, God's relationship to Israel and her king is seen
in terms of the covenant relationship and its potential for
blessing or cursing.

A brief word is necessary on the Deuteronomistic conception of the role of Samuel in chapters 7-15. Samuel appears in
the Deuteronomistic material only in chapters 8 and 12, both
times in connection with a large assembly of the people. Muilenburg has emphasized Samuel's role in chapter 12 as a covenant mediator similar to Moses and Joshua.[10] This is certainly
an element in the Deuteronomistic conception of Samuel. In
12:6-15, a passage reflecting the covenantal form, Samuel presents the covenant demands to the people. The scene is reminiscent of Joshua at Shechem in Jos. 24 where the covenant is
renewed. There is, however, more to Samuel's role here than
that of covenant mediator. We have already noted that 12:19-24

represents a homiletical reflection on the themes introduced in the covenantal speech of 12:6-15. Here the dominant theme is exhortation to faithfulness following the people's confession in vs. 19. In short, the style is sermonic and Samuel is a preacher. The same might be said of the Deuteronomistic picture of Samuel in chapter 8. Here, rather than exhorting the people to faithfulness, Samuel is warning them of the potential danger which lies before them, but again the style is sermonic and Samuel's role here is best conceived as a preacher. It is clear that this view of Samuel is not greatly different than the picture of Moses in the parenetic portions of Deuteronomy.[11] There Moses preaches to the people, exhorting them to faithfulness and obedience and warning against the potential dangers awaiting them in the land they are about to enter. It should also be noted that in Deuteronomy, too, Moses appears as the covenant mediator (Deut. 5) and as in 12:19 acts as an intercessor for the people (Deut. 9). One other element must be added to the Deuteronomistic conception of Samuel's role in chapters 7-15. In 12:11, the Deuteronomist apparently considers Samuel to be one of the charismatic heroes who delivered Israel in a time of crisis. This role, mentioned without further expansion or elaboration, is unexpected in connection with Samuel's role as covenant mediator and preacher. It may, in fact, rise from the Deuteronomistic supplements to chapter 7 which, as we have seen, are intended to incorporate the victory over the Philistines in chapter 7 into the framework of sin/repentance/delivery known to us from the Book of Judges. It is clear that in the old tradition itself (7:7ff.), Samuel is not a deliverer, and the Deuteronomist has not altered this old account. However, it is possible that in the historical retrospect of chapter 12, the Deuteronomist, counting this victory in the series of deliverances, included Samuel as the deliverer in order to complete his schema. In any case, Samuel as a deliverer plays a small role in the Deuteronomistic picture.

It is impossible to say much concerning the date and setting of the Deuteronomistic history work on the basis of his work in I Sam. 7-15. It is clear from the previous analysis of

the material that his work constitutes the last literary level
in the development of the material. At the current stage of
debate, this would allow it to be dated anywhere from the reign
of Josiah in the late seventh century to the period of the
exile around 550 B.C.[12] Many scholars have claimed that the
anti-monarchical views of I Sam. 8 and 12 support an exilic
date for the work of the Deuteronomist. Although the question
lies beyond this study, we would at least point out that the
Deuteronomistic material in chapters 8 and 12 still holds out
the possibility of the blessing as well as the curse. Further,
material earlier than the Deuteronomistic work shows a decidedly positive attitude toward David and yet are left untouched by
the Deuteronomist.[13]

III

At this point, we have distinguished both the first and
the last stages in the process of growth through which chapters
7-15 came into their present shape. The crucial question which
remains is the nature of any intervening stages. The analysis
of the individual chapters has shown obvious evidence at many
points of materials which lie intermediate between the old traditions on the one hand and the work of the Deuteronomist on
the other. Some of these materials have made conscious use of
the older traditions (e.g. 9:1-10:16) so that this intermediate
stage of development may be considered to involve the editing
of old traditions as well as the adding of new materials. The
chief question before us then becomes whether these evidences
of intermediate editorial activity are isolated from one
another or form a single, unified edition composed of old traditions edited and ordered together with materials from the
editor's own hand. We believe the latter to be the case and
shall attempt in what follows to identify those circles from
which this edition came and the theological perspective which
the edition is intended to support.

There are several reasons for advancing the hypothesis of
a complete edition of the materials in chapters 7-15 prior to
the work of the Deuteronomist. There are some direct connections between various passages. The anointing in 10:1 is

re-echoed in 12:3, 5 and 15:1, 17. The first rejection of Saul
in 13:7b-15a recalls the command of Samuel in 10:8. The opponents of Saul in 10:27 seem to provide the basis for the episode in 11:12-13. However, it must be stressed that these
minor connections are in themselves far from sufficient evidence for the existence of a pre-Deuteronomistic edition, although they might lend some support to the hypothesis.

One of the major reasons for suspecting a prior edition is
the already mentioned supplementary nature of the Deuteronomistic work in chapters 7-15. It is well known that the Deuteronomist engaged in extensive ordering and editing of his source
material in the Books of Judges and Kings. It is also acknowl-
edged by most that his work is less extensive in the Books of
Samuel because he encountered some already existing collections
of material which he used (e.g. the Succession History in II
Sam. 9-20). It would seem but a small step to suggest that in
I Sam. 7-15 the Deuteronomist also found an already existing
edition of the tradition materials concerning the rise of the
Israelite kingship and confined his activity to a few supplementary additions and the programmatic speech in chapter 12 to
conclude the period of the league. The strongest argument for
the existence of a pre-Deuteronomistic edition of chapters 7-15
is the organization of these materials to promote a specific
theological view of this period in Israel's history. However,
before taking up this question, we should ask what evidence
there is for identifying those circles in which such an edition
might arise. This will allow us better to understand the theological views which motivate the edition.

Certain passages show clearly that the pre-Deuteronomistic
edition stems from early prophetic circles.[14] For the most
part, these are the materials which have been completely shaped
by what we shall call the prophetic editor. These passages may
be listed as follows:

     9:15-17, 20-21, (25-26), 27-10:1(LXX), 5-8, 16b
     10:17-19, 25
     11:12-14
     12:1-5
     13:7b-15a
     15:1-35

Our analyses of these passages have shown some of them to be shaped around formal types long recognized as stemming from the early prophetic community. The anointing of Saul by Samuel in 9:15-17, 20-21, (25-26), 27-10:1(LXX), 5-8, 16b is influenced by the form of the prophetic call narrative. The presence of the prophetic judgment speech to an individual is apparent in the two accounts of Saul's sin and rejection (13:7b-15a and 15:1-35). Samuel's speech prior to the choice of Saul by lot in 10:17-19 shows the pattern of the prophetic judgment speech to the nation. All of these passages show the influence of formal types, the setting of which our analysis has clearly traced to prophetic circles. Further, these passages do not simply represent additional tradition material alongside the older traditions listed earlier. ⟨The prophetic editor shows that he knows these older traditions and has used them in various ways.⟩ In chapters 9 and 10, the editor has taken an old folk tale of Saul's search for the asses and used it as the occasion for an expansion from his own material telling of Samuel's anointing of Saul. In 10:17ff., the old tradition fragment of Saul's choice by lot is preceded by the oracle of judgment, the announcement of which is replaced by the old tradition, thus placing it in quite a different light. The narrative of Saul's rejection from dynasty in 13:7bff. is inserted into the collection of materials on Saul's Philistine military ventures in order to provide a proper setting for the account. Chapter 15, the account of Saul's rejection from the kingship, does not make use of any older material but serves to conclude the episode of Saul's rise and fall. As a further example of the technique of the prophetic editor, we might mention the harmonizing note of 11:14 which serves to reconcile the existence of two coronation accounts. This brief survey of results previously reported in our analysis of the chapters makes clear that the prophetic editor responsible for the passages listed on the previous page also made extensive use of the older traditions before him. Some of these older traditions, as we have seen, have been altered in some way by the insertion or juxtaposition of the prophetic editor's own material. However, others (e.g. chapter 11) have remained untouched, but it is our

contention that they have been placed in their present order by
the prophetic editor in order to play a role in his theological
schema. In short, except for the Deuteronomistic additions,
the prophetic editor is responsible for the arrangement of all
the rest of the material in chapters 7-15 in order to advance
his own theological position in reference to these traditions.
At a later point we will discuss the role played by all of
these materials in the theological program of the prophetic
editor.

The formal types represented in the list of passages on
the previous page have helped us to identify their provenance
as prophetic, but they can also further aid us in establishing
a more specific time period within the large period of prophetic activity. The analysis of 13:7bff. and chapter 15 showed
the influence of the judgment speech to an individual, and in
general, this speech form disappears shortly after the beginning of the period of the writing prophets.[15] However, it was
also seen that both of these passages show a grammatical causal
connection between the accusation and the announcement, which
is a late development in the form. Thus, we can tentatively
date the two passages to a period close to the beginning of the
period of the writing prophets (perhaps the last half of the
eighth century B.C.). On the other hand, 10:17-19 is influenced by the form of the judgment speech to the nation, a form
more common to the writing prophets. However, here is found
the motif contrasting God's deed in the past with Israel's
present sin. Westermann points out that this is an early form
of the contrast since the later development stresses also Israel's rebellion in the past.[16] Further, this motif of contrast is the only expansion of the form which is also present
in the form of the judgment speech to an individual. Thus, it
is entirely possible that 10:17-19 stems from a time early in
the period of the writing prophets which overlaps with the period in which the form of the judgment to an individual was
still alive. Thus, on the basis of form, a tentative dating to
the last half of the eighth century B.C. is possible. This
general time period would also be suitable for the use of the
form of the prophetic call narrative in chapters 9-10.

The positing of an early prophetic provenance for the pre-Deuteronomistic edition of I Samuel 7-15 is supported by a consideration of the portrayal of Samuel in that material which we have argued stems from the hand of the prophetic editor. In his utterances and actions, Samuel appears as a prophet in this material. This picture of Samuel as a prophet accords well with the information that can be gathered concerning the activities of the pre-writing prophets such as Nathan, Ahijah and Elijah. Thus, the circles which portrayed Samuel in this manner cannot date long after the end of the period in which the pre-writing prophets were active. We must now turn to an examination of the various elements in this picture of Samuel and a comparison of these elements with other sources for early Hebrew prophetism.

1. In I Sam. 9:15-17, 20-21 (25-26), 27-10:1(LXX), 5-8, 16b, Samuel acts as the agent of God in designating and anointing Saul. Here the use of the form of the prophetic call narrative alone would direct us to assume that the account stems from prophetic circles. However, there is ample evidence that several kings in the northern kingdom were designated by prophets, thus making clear that Samuel's role here is intended to be a prophetic one. In I Kgs. 11:29ff., Ahijah designated Jeroboam as king over the breakaway northern tribes. Similarly, Baasha, who exterminated the house of Jeroboam, was apparently raised to power by prophetic designation (I Kgs. 16:1). Perhaps the closest parallel to Samuel's activity is to be seen in connection with the rise of Jehu to the kingship bringing the fall of the Omride dynasty. In I Kgs. 19:15-16, Elijah is commanded by God to anoint Jehu as king (as well as to anoint Elisha as his successor). Elijah does not carry out this task himself, but in II Kgs. 9 at the instigation of Elisha one of the "sons of the prophets" carries out the anointing. Alt[17] has indicated that we must see in this practice a continuation of the "charismatic" understanding of the military leader in the amphictyony.[18] Thus, Samuel and the other early prophets may be considered as the agents of God's designating charisma. In the account of the anointing of Saul by Samuel, this is followed by the possession of the spirit (as it is also in the

anointing of David, 16:13). Samuel's act then becomes a prophetic endowment of the spirit, a phenomenon which von Rad points out is seen in the time of Elijah but fades from sight in the period of classical prophecy.[19]

2. In I Sam. 13:7b-15a and 15:1-35, Samuel pronounces judgment over Saul's claim to dynasty and his claim to the kingship in accounts marked by their formal dependence on the prophetic speech form of the judgment speech to an individual. The clearest parallels to Samuel's actions here are again to be found among the pre-classical prophets. Jeroboam and Baasha, having been designated like Saul by prophets, are both rejected from the kingship by prophetic judgment (I Kgs. 14:7f. and 16: 1ff.). The prophets were also responsible for bringing the Omride dynasty to an end and designating its successor (II Kgs. 9:30-10:11). Besides these instances of prophets' bringing kingships to an end, there are numerous examples of the prophetic confrontation of kings with their violations of God's law. The prophet appears as the defender of God's law, and as God's messenger he delivers God's judgments on those kings who fail to carry out God's commands.[20] Wolff and Westermann have both argued persuasively that the form of the judgment speech to an individual is patterned on the regular court procedure.[21] The king, however, is exempt from the actions of the common court, and it is the prophet who announces that he has not escaped divine judgment. Nathan confronts David with his sin in II Sam. 12. Elijah reproaches Ahab in the matter of Naboth's vineyard in I Kgs. 21. Gad announces God's judgment on David in II Sam. 24. The clearest parallel to the role of Samuel in our material, however, stands in I Kgs. 20:35ff. where an unnamed prophet pronounces judgment on Yahweh's behalf upon Ahab for failing to carry out the commandment of destruction in the holy war and allowing Ben-hadad to live. It is in a precisely similar role that Samuel appears in chapter 15. Thus, it might now be seen that Samuel appears here in the prophetic role of the watchman over God's law and the messenger of the divine court. In passing, it might be noted that this prophetic, yet judicial, role could have appeared to the prophetic editor as not inconsistent with the older traditions' portrayal of Samuel

as a judge. Indeed, Noth and Rendtorff have both pointed out
that the connection of judicial and charismatic functions may
not have been entirely uncommon.[22] In any case, Samuel's role
as a prophetic guardian of the law can be clearly seen in the
pre-Deuteronomistic edition.

3. Although it has been briefly mentioned in connection
with earlier matters, it should be pointed out that at the same
time that Samuel is delivering God's judgment on Saul for his
misdeeds he is in both 13:7bff. and 15:1ff. serving as the pre-
server of the amphictyonic institution of the holy war. The
prophets often appear on the battlefield beside the armies of
Israel to advise the king and to demand that the wars be carried out according to the sacral principles of the holy war
(I Kgs. 20:13-14, 22, 28, 35f.; II Kgs. 3:11f.; 13:14f.). Many
have recognized in the references to Elijah and Elisha as "the
chariots of Israel and its horsemen" (II Kgs. 2:12; 13:14) a
reference to their connection with the ideology of holy war.
In a recent study, Bach has emphasized the prophets as the pre-
servers of amphictyonic tradition. In connection with the holy
war, he concludes that the traditions of the holy war were
taken up into prophecy already at the time of the establishment
of the state or immediately thereafter.[23] Certainly Samuel appears in the prophetic role of the protector of the holy war
ideology in 13:7bff. and 15:1ff. It is also worthy of note
that the proposed prophetic edition also makes prominent use of
older traditions which relate to the holy war (chapters 7, 11,
14). In chapter 11, the spirit which comes upon Saul is, by
its position following chapter 10, made to seem related to that
which possessed Saul in connection with his prophetic anointment. It is also interesting to note that chapter 7 portrays
Samuel as playing the key role in the holy war rituals which
precede the sending of the divine panic on the enemy.[24]

These elements in the portrayal of Samuel, added to the
use of prophetic speech forms placed in the mouth of Samuel,
make it apparent that the pre-Deuteronomistic edition of chapters 7-15 pictures Samuel as a prophet similar to those who
were active toward the end of the period of the divided monarchy. This in turn supports our contention that the circles

responsible for this edition are to be found in prophetic circles dating not later than the late eighth century.

The view of the kingship in the prophetic edition of I Samuel 7-15 is greatly influenced by the claim that he assumes his office through prophetic designation. This view certainly differs greatly from the wary tolerance with which the Deuteronomist regards the king. It is also decidedly different from the tendency of some of the older traditions to emphasize Saul as a heroic figure (e.g. his stature and beauty, 9:2; 10:23, his heroic deeds, chapter 11). For the prophetic editor, the king stands in a special relationship to God because he is primarily viewed as God's anointed. God has designated him through anointing by his prophet, and commissioned him to lead his people. This is, of course, seen most clearly in the anointing account itself in chapters 9-10, but it also appears elsewhere. In 12:3 and 5, the king is referred to as God's anointed and coupled with him as the ultimate source of appeal in judicial matters. Even more important, the whole account of Saul's rejection is placed in the framework of his position as God's anointed in 15:1. Saul's rejection is due to his failure to take seriously enough his special position before God. In his attempts to indict the people for the misdeed (vss. 15, 24) it is made clear to him that it is he, as king, who bore the authority of God and therefore must be held responsible (15:17, 26). It might be well to emphasize again that Saul appears as God's anointed only in the prophetic material and not in the old tradition material or the Deuteronomistic additions.

The special position of the king is also emphasized by seeing him as one possessed by the spirit of God. Following his anointing, Saul is seized by the spirit in an encounter with a prophetic band precisely as Samuel had indicated he would be (10:5ff.). Interestingly, Saul's first public act in the present arrangement of the materials is motivated by the possession of God's spirit (chapter 11). In the analysis, it was seen that this view of spirit possession stems from a different setting, but in the present arrangement of material it is hard not to view chapter 11 as the public functioning of the spirit which serves to confirm Saul as one so possessed. An even stronger piece of evidence for the thesis that the king is here regarded as one possessed by the spirit can be seen in chapter 16. Here the first remark made concerning Saul following his rejection in chapter 15 is that the spirit of Yahweh left him (16:14). This is immediately preceded in vs. 13 by the notice of David's anointing which is followed by the statement that he was subsequently possessed by the spirit of Yahweh.

The special position of the king before God in the prophetic edition also brings with it a special responsibility before God. The king was not subject to the authority of normal judicial institutions but is instead subject to divine justice. This view was particularly prominent in early prophetic circles where, as we have seen, it was the prophet's duty to confront the king with the divine judgments rendered against his transgressions.[25] It is clearly Saul's failure to fulfill his special responsibilities before the divine law that results in his rejection in chapter 15. Von Rad has come closest to stating this when he writes, "The picture of Saul certainly makes it clear that the life of the anointed was still subject to other laws than was the life of the ordinary human beings, and that it was threatened by the possibility of much more dreadful disaster."[26] It is, however, not only in Saul's rejection that the prophetic editor shows his concern for the king's obligations before divine law. In 10:25, it is Samuel who writes the משפט המלכה in a book and places it in the sanctuary after having announced it publicly. Thus, it is made clear that Saul could not have been unaware of his special position of responsibility before God's law. Briefly, the picture of the king which emerges from I Sam. 7-15 in the pre-Deuteronomistic, prophetic edition is that the king stands in a special relationship to God as his anointed and the bearer of his spirit. As such, he is also the bearer of special responsibilities in the fulfillment of the divine law, and it is Saul's failure in this respect that brings him to grief. It might be added that it is David (also God's anointed and the bearer of his spirit) who does not fail in his obedience to the divine law, and his kingdom is ultimately the recipient of special blessing (II Sam. 7).

The question must now be raised as to whether it is possible to posit an organizing principle or theological program
which can adequately explain the bringing together of such a
diverse group of old traditions and later prophetic materials.
The first assertion that might be made is that the editor seems
to have organized his material around a systematic presentation
of the career of God's anointed.[27] Rolf Knierim writes that
"Old Testament historians occasionally employ a technique of
composition in which an account of a vocation is followed by a
narrative which is intended to demonstrate the functioning of
the charisma which is bestowed in the vocation."[28] This technique is apparent in the material on the rise of Saul to the
kingship. The entire section of material might be said to be
based on the theology of divine charisma as it relates to God's
anointed. In 9:1-10:16 is the account of Saul's election by
Yahweh through anointing by the prophet Samuel. Following the
anointing, Saul receives the spirit of God. The next stage in
the career of the anointed is his public presentation, which is
accomplished in 10:17-27 with his elevation to the kingship at
the assembly of all Israel. This is then followed by the public functioning of the charisma. In chapter 11, Saul, possessed by the spirit, accomplishes a miraculous victory over the
Ammonites after which his kingship is reaffirmed. His victory
constitutes the proof of his charisma.[29] Chapter 12 is, of
course, a later Deuteronomistic interruption of the prophetic
editor's organized presentation. Chapters 13-15 constitute the
record of Saul's failure as God's anointed. While carrying out
those military tasks which were a part of his commission as the
anointed, he fails in the test of complete obedience, and
through prophetically-delivered judgment he is rejected both
from future dynasty and from the kingship itself. The next
mention of Saul tells us that the spirit left him and was replaced by an evil spirit (16:14). Saul thus ceases to be the
holder of the charisma. That this general structure represents
an intentional ordering of materials can best be seen by comparing it briefly to the ordering of the materials on David.
Here a similar pattern can be detected tracing David's career
as God's anointed and the possessor of his spirit, although

with important and purposeful differences. David's election,
anointing by Samuel and possession of the spirit are recorded
in 16:1-13 immediately following Saul's rejection. Both of the
rejection stories foreshadowed this rise of David. David's
public presentation is to be seen in his presentation at the
court of Saul in 16:14-23, which is ironically linked to the
need for Saul to have someone to soothe him when tormented by
the evil spirit which now possesses him. The public functioning of the charisma for David is found in the battle with
Goliath in chapter 17 and serves to confirm David as a man possessed of charisma in the people's eyes. His rising popularity
with the people is recorded in 18:6ff. The whole of chapters
18:1-27:4 is concerned now with the conflict and rivalry between the two who have been anointed, one dispossessed of the
spirit and the other possessing it. This section also serves
as the testing of David which he passes whereas Saul was found
guilty. David's innocence is stressed at numerous points in
the account (I Sam. 19:4-5; 20:1, 8; 24:4-22; 25:32-34; 26:8-
25; 27:8-11; 29:4ff.; 30:17ff., 23ff.). David's innocence as
compared to Saul's guilt is already hinted at in 15:28. Chapters 27:5-31:13 record the death of Saul, and David, who stood
the test, is confirmed in the kingship and given the blessing
of dynasty (II Sam. 7), those very things from which Saul was
rejected.

Of course, I Sam. 7 and 8 cannot be said to concern the
career of God's anointed; however, they do play an important
preparatory role in the organization of I Sam. 7-15. Most
scholars are now in agreement that the tradition of the people's request for a king is a genuinely old one even though
chapter 8 as we now have it has been reshaped by the Deuteronomist. It is probable that the prophetic editor also knew this
tradition, but interestingly he follows that tradition with the
account of Saul's anointing which took place when Saul was a
youth. The implication is that the people were not influencing
God's will, for God had long before foreseen the coming of the
kingship and designated Saul. A similar emphasis on the su-
premacy of God's will was seen in the analysis of the editor's
use of the lot-casting tradition. A special word must be said

on the old tradition of I Sam. 8:1-7 since it introduces the
only note of tension into the enthusiastic view of Saul's
choice as king in the prophetic edition. We have characterized
the viewpoint of the old tradition in chapter 8 as a "sinful-
but-still-of-God" view of the kingship, and it is found only in
this one place in the old traditions. Its presence in the
prophetic edition, however, need not be seen as a locating of
the old pro- and anti-monarchical tension in a later pre-Deuteronomistic stage. It is merely witness to the existence of
a less than enthusiastic viewpoint of kingship at the time of
the events themselves.[30] The prophetic editor shows his aware-
ness of this tension by his attempt to deal with it directly
in 10:17ff. where the editor leads us up to an implied judgment
against the people and replaces the announcement of that judgment with an old tradition emphasizing the working of God's
providence in selecting Saul and ending on a note of enthusiastic proclamation of his kingship. All other passages usually
attributed to an anti-monarchical source can be seen as either
passages reflecting Saul's failure as God's anointed (therefore
judgment against Saul and not the kingship) or as later Deuteronomistic additions. This diverse group of materials could
hardly be called a source.

Chapter 7 must also be seen as a protection of the sovereign will of God. The fact of a grave Philistine military crisis is as firmly rooted in the tradition as the request of the
people. However, in the present arrangement of material, chapter 7 records a decisive victory over the Philistines before a
king had been chosen. Just as the anointing of Saul as a youth
removes the danger of seeing the people's request as a coercion
of God, the victory in chapter 7 removes the danger of seeing a
king as the only means of delivering Israel from the Philistines. The present editorial arrangement then serves to emphasize the kingship as an act of graciousness on the part of God,
and not as an act into which Israel was forced out of necessity. Since the Deuteronomistic materials are additions to
these chapters, and since the present arrangement of chapters
7-8 accords well with the emphasis on the sovereign working of
God's will in the following chapters, it would seem most

likely that the position of these chapters can be attributed to
the prophetic editor. The prophetic edition is concerned to
understand the careers of Saul and David in terms of their
position as God's anointed and the possessors of his spirit,
but underlying this is a constant emphasis on the primacy of
God's will in effecting these events.

What might have been the historical situation that called
forth a prophetic edition such as has been described above?
Such questions must necessarily border on the speculative, but
a brief consideration is in order. What has already been said
regarding the date of the prophetic edition might be profitably
reviewed. In form, the materials seem to date to the latter
half of the eighth century when the older form of the judgment
to an individual was still current but early judgment forms
most characteristic of the writing prophets could already be
detected. This period would accord well with the picture of
Samuel which best fits that of the northern prophets of the
divided monarchy. The picture of the king also accords better
with that of the kings of the northern kingdom rather than with
those of the Davidic dynasty. Hence, the prophetic edition
cannot date much later than the fall of Israel in 721 nor much
earlier than the emergence of classical prophetic forms in the
last half of the eighth century. Further, the circles from
which it came seem to be those of northern prophetic tradition,
especially in light of the traditions of the prophetic designation of kings. However, as we have seen, the concern of this
edition is to demonstrate the failure of Saul to filfill the
obligations of his charismatic designation, and this is done in
conscious contrast to David who succeeds and is blessed. The
southern Davidic dynasty is thus legitimized in charismatic
terms more characteristic of the northern kingdom. We would
suggest that the most logical explanation is that the prophetic
edition dates to the period immediately following the fall of
Samaria in the late eighth century B.C. From this point on-
wards, Yahwistic prophecy is centered entirely in the south,
although it continues to possess links to tradition complexes
which are essentially northern. Since the fall of Samaria con-
stituted a clear confirmation of the Davidic kingdom over

against that of the north, it was necessary that this event be understood theologically. For those prophetic circles still oriented toward the charismatic understanding of the kingship and the corresponding importance of the prophet's role in relation to that kingship, the Saul-David traditions provided an obvious theological justification for the events of 721. Saul, a northern king, was indeed chosen by God, but he failed in obedience and was rejected. It was David, representing the southern kingdom, who received the blessing of eternal kingship. Although it lies beyond the scope of this study, it may well be that evidence of a prophetic edition which pre-dates the Deuteronomist can be found in the remainder of the Books of Samuel and possibly in certain portions of the Books of Kings.

A brief final word must be said concerning the relationship of the prophetic edition which has been proposed and the work of the Deuteronomist. The Deuteronomistic material has already been seen as essentially supplementary in nature, whereas extensive evidence of his activity is present in the Books of Judges and Kings. We would suggest that the Deuteronomist found himself basically sympathetic to the emphases of the prophetic edition he had before him and therefore found extensive editorial work unnecessary. Certainly it is well known that Deuteronomy itself is believed to show evidence of prophetic influence. It has even been suggested that Deuteronomy originated in the north.[31] In any case, emphasis on Saul's disobedience and David's obedience would suit the Deuteronomist's covenantal theme of blessing and cursing very well, and in fact he introduces it in chapter 12. For the most part, the Deuteronomist is concerned only to paint a less positive picture of the king than that of the prophetic editor, and most of his additions are to that end. He is willing to incorporate into his overall schema the remainder of the prophetic edition in essentially its original form.

In conclusion, the process of growth and development through which I Samuel 7-15 came into its present shape can be summarized as follows:

A. The events surrounding the establishment of the Israelite monarchy produced a rich variety of traditions which

seem, for the most part, to have circulated independently of
one another. Except for a small collection of materials on
Saul's military ventures in chapters 13-14, there is no evidence that these materials came together in sources of any
sort.

 B. A pre-Deuteronomistic editor is responsible for bringing these diverse traditions together into a single edition
along with other materials bearing his own peculiar stamp (9:
15-17, 20-21, 27-10:1, 5-8, 16b; 10:17-19, 25; 11:12-14; 12:1-
5; 13:7b-15a; 15:1-35). The nature of the editor's own materials provides the best clue to his identity as prophetic, and
the schema underlying the overall arrangement supports that
identification. The edition may be attributed to northern
prophetic circles in the late eighth century B.C. probably following the fall of Samaria in 721.

 C. The Deuteronomistic historian has incorporated the
earlier prophetic edition into his history work with only a few
additions (7:3-4, 13-14; 8:8, 10-22; 12:6-24; 13:1). Included
here is a typical speech by Samuel in chapter 12 to end the
period of the tribal league. This work dates at least as late
as the time of Josiah (our study provides too small a basis for
speculation on an exact date for the Deuteronomistic work).
Although painting a dimmer view of kingship, he is for the most
part in sympathy with the tone of the prophetic edition and
allows it to stand relatively untouched.

[1]It should be noted that this list does not exclude the possibility that other materials have their roots in genuinely old tradition. The list merely indicates those passages in which old traditions or tradition fragments can be distinguished from the work of later hands.

[2]The folk tale of Saul's search for the asses cannot be considered to be a third account since it does not in fact tell of Saul's becoming king. In the old folk tale, the point was seen to be a miraculous foretelling of Saul's future greatness.

[3]The release of Samuel from blame in rendering judgments in 12:1-5 may also have its *Sitz* in the tradition of Samuel as a judge.

[4]Martin Noth, "Das Amt des 'Richters Israels'," *Festschrift für A. Bertholet*, (1950), pp. 404-417, and "Office and Vocation in the Old Testament," *The Laws in the Pentateuch and Other Essays*, p. 244. A similar conclusion is reached by G. von Rad, *Old Testament Theology*, vol. I, p. 42; Hans Wildberger, "Samuel und die Entstehung des israelitischen Königtums," *TZ*, 13 (1957), pp. 442ff.; and A. Weiser, "Samuels 'Philister-Sieg': Die Überlieferungen in I Sam. 7," *ZThK*, 56 (1959), pp. 253ff.

[5]Weiser, *op. cit.*, p. 269.

[6]It is not our intention to discuss the wider issues involved in the hypothesis of a Deuteronomistic history work. Our limited goal is to discuss the methods and viewpoint of only those passages within chapters 7-15 of I Samuel which can be identified as Deuteronomistic. This will naturally give a less than complete picture of the Deuteronomistic work as a whole, but might have some bearing on that picture. For the classic treatment of the hypothesis of a Deuteronomistic history work, see Martin Noth, *Überlieferungsgeschichtliche Studien*.

[7]For a general overview of the major motifs in Deuteronomy and the Deuteronomistic history work, see E. W. Nicholson, *Deuteronomy and Tradition*, (Philadelphia: Fortress Press, 1967); and G. von Rad, *Deuteronomy*, (Philadelphia: Westminster Press, 1966), and *Studies in Deuteronomy*, "Studies in Biblical Theology," no. 9 (London: SCM Press, 1953).

[8]Von Rad, *Deuteronomy*, p. 119. See also A. Alt, "Die Heimat des Deuteronomiums," *Kleine Schriften*, vol. II, (1959), p. 264.

[9]Although it lies beyond the scope of this study, the Deuteronomist's attitude toward David might be a profitable study

in connection with this matter. F. M. Cross, "The Structure of the Deuteronomic History," *Perspectives in Jewish Learning*, vol. 3, edited by J. M. Rosenthal, (Chicago: College of Jewish Studies Press, 1967), has suggested that David, as the proto-type of the ideally obedient king, is an important element in the Deuteronomistic theology of the Books of Kings. It may well be that the idea of blessing through the king plays a more prominent role in the Deuteronomistic history than is usually recognized.

[10] James Muilenburg, "The Form and Structure of the Cove-nantal Formulations," *VT*, 9 (1959), pp. 347-65.

[11] This similarity has been studied at length by Austin David Ritterspach, *The Samuel Traditions: An Analysis of the Anti-Monarchical Source in I Sam. 1-15*, unpublished disserta-tion, Graduate Theological Union, 1967.

[12] See Nicholson, *op. cit.*, pp. 113ff.

[13] One might also call to mind the extremely positive eval-uation of Josiah in II Kgs. 23:25 which many scholars agree should be attributed the Deuteronomist.

[14] It is hoped that the sense in which we use this phrase will emerge more clearly as the discussion progresses.

[15] Westermann, *Basic Forms of Prophetic Speech*, p. 138.

[16] *Ibid.*, p. 183.

[17] A. Alt, "The Monarchy in Israel and Judah," *Essays on Old Testament History and Religion*, translated by R. A. Wilson (Oxford: Basil Blackwell, 1966), pp. 239ff.

[18] This may also be seen in I Sam. 9-10 in the use of the term נגיד (vss. 9:16 and 10:1).

[19] G. von Rad, *Old Testament Theology*, vol. II, p. 56.

[20] R. Rendtorff, "Reflections on the Early History of Prophecy in Israel," *History and Hermeneutics*, edited by Robert Funk, p. 26: "Precisely this function of the prophets as watch-men of God's law belongs even form-critically, in all probabil-ity, to the oldest elements of the history of Israelite prophe-cy."

[21] H. W. Wolff, *Das Zitat im Prophetenspruch* (Munich: C. Kaiser, 1937); Westermann, *Basic Forms of Prophetic Speech*, p. 136. Their work has been supported by the more recent work of H. J. Boecker, *Redeformen des Rechtslebens im Alten Testament* (Neukirchen: Neukirchener Verlag, 1964).

[22] Rendtorff, *op. cit.*, p. 30. M. Noth, "Office and Voca-tion in the Old Testament," *The Laws in the Pentateuch and Other Essays*, p. 244.

[23]R. Bach, *Die Aufforderungen zur Flucht und zum Kampf im alttestamentlichen Prophetenspruch*, p. 112.

[24]Of course, it is well known that Deuteronomy is also concerned with the institution of holy war. However, the absence of any significant role in the holy war for either king or prophet (see von Rad, *Studies in Deuteronomy*, p. 51) rules out any possibility that the holy war traditions of I Sam. 7; 11; 13:7bff.; 14; or 15 stem from a Deuteronomistic hand. In all of these, Saul or Samuel play a significant role in either carrying out the holy war demands or guarding against their violation. In the "ordinances which Deuteronomy reintroduced, there is at work a strong tendency towards the reinstitution of what obtained in the past," von Rad, *op. cit.* The holy war traditions of I Sam. 7-15 more closely reflect the period of the divided monarchy.

[25]See the discussion in Westermann, *op. cit.*, pp. 133ff.

[26]G. von Rad, *Old Testament Theology*, vol. I, p. 325.

[27]A similar conclusion regarding the organizing principle of the pre-Deuteronomistic book of I Samuel was reached independently by R. Knierim in an article entitled "The Messianic Concept in the First Book of Samuel," *Jesus and the Historian*, edited by F. Thomas Trotter. Knierim has followed this messianic principle on through the David materials, and I am indebted to him for suggestions on the analogies between the Saul and David material on the matter of the career of God's anointed.

[28]Knierim, *op. cit.*, p. 26.

[29]Von Rad, *op. cit.*, p. 329, writes that in the accounts of Gideon, Jephthah, Samson and Saul, "the call is followed immediately by the public proof of the charisma effected by means of a victory over the enemy."

[30]A growing number of scholars have suggested that the tradition preserved in I Sam. 8:1-7 must be given greater historical value. See note 35, p. 113. Most recently this notion has been argued by Austin David Ritterspach, *The Samuel Traditions*; see note 11, p. 156.

[31]See the discussion in Nicholson, *Deuteronomy and Tradition*, pp. 58ff.

BIBLIOGRAPHY

Aharoni, Yohanan. *The Land of the Bible*, translated by A. F.
Rainey. Philadelphia: Westminster, 1967.

Ahlström, G. W. "Die Königsideologie in Israel. Ein Dis-
kussionsbeitrag," *TZ*, 18 (1962), pp. 205ff.

Albright, W. F. *Archaeology, Historical Analogy and Early
Biblical Tradition*. Baton Rouge: Louisiana State University Press, 1966.

_____. *From the Stone Age to Christianity*. Garden City,
N.Y.: Doubleday, 1957.

_____. *Samuel and the Beginnings of the Prophetic Movement*.
Cincinnati: Hebrew Union College Press, 1961.

Alonso-Schökel, L. "Erzählkunst im Buche der Richter," *Biblica*, 42 (1961), pp. 143ff.

Alt, Albrecht. *Essays on Old Testament History and Religion*,
translated by R. A. Wilson. Oxford: Basil Blackwell,
1966.

_____. "Saul," *RGG^2*, vol. 5 (1931), col. 120f.

_____. "Die Wallfahrt von Sichem nach Bethel," *Kleine
Schriften zur Geschichte des Volkes Israel*, vol. 1.
München: C. H. Beck, 1953.

_____. "Zu II Sam. 8:1," *ZAW*, 54 (1936), pp. 149ff.

Anderson, B. W. *The Office of the Judge in the Old Testament*.
Yale Dissertation, 1945.

Ap-Thomas, D. R. "Saul's Uncle," *VT*, 11 (1961), pp. 241-45.

Baars, W. "A Forgotten Fragment of the Greek Text of the Books
of Samuel," *Oudtestamentische Studien*, 14 (1965), pp. 201-
05.

Bach, R. *Die Aufforderungen zur Flucht und zum Kampf im alttestamentlichen Prophetenspruch*. Neukirchen: Neukirchener
Verlag, 1962.

Beer, Georg. *Saul, David, Salomo*. Tübingen: J.C.B. Mohr,
1906.

Bentzen, Aage. "The Cultic Use of the Story of the Ark in
Samuel," *JBL*, 67 (1948), pp. 37-53.

_____. *Introduction to the Old Testament*, vol. II, second
edition. Copenhagen: G.E.C. Gad, 1952.

159

Beyerlin, Walter. "Das Königscharisma bei Saul," *ZAW*, 73 (1961), pp. 186ff.

_____. *Origins and History of the Oldest Sinaitic Traditions*. Translated by S. Rudman. Oxford: Basil Blackwell, 1965.

Bič, Miloš. "Saul sucht die Eselinnen (I Sam. IX)," *VT*, 7 (1957), pp. 92-97.

Blenkinsopp, J. "Are There Traces of the Gibeonite Covenant in Deuteronomy?" *CBQ*, 28 (1966), pp. 207ff.

_____. "Jonathan's Sacrilege," *CBQ*, 26 (1964), pp. 423-49.

_____. "Structure and Style in Jdgs. 13-16," *JBL*, 82 (1963), pp. 65ff.

Boecker, Hans Jochen. *Redeformen des Rechtslebens im Alten Testament*. Neukirchen: Neukirchener Verlag, 1964.

de Boer, P. A. H. "Research into the Text of I Sam. 18-31," *Oudtestamentische Studien*, 6 (1949), pp. 1-100.

_____. "Vive le Roi," *VT*, 5 (1955), pp. 225-31.

Bright, John. "I and II Samuel," *Interpretation*, 5 (1951), pp. 450ff.

_____. *A History of Israel*. Philadelphia: Westminster, 1959.

Buber, Martin. "Die Erzählung von Sauls Königswahl," *VT*, 6 (1956), pp. 113ff.

_____. *The Kingship of God*. New York: Harper and Row, 1967.

Budde, Karl. *Die Bücher Richter und Samuel, ihre Quellen und ihre Aufbau*. Tübingen: J.C.B. Mohr, 1890.

_____. *Die Bücher Samuel*. Tübingen: J.C.B. Mohr, 1902.

_____. "Saul's Königswahl und Verwerfung," *ZAW*, 8 (1888), pp. 223ff.

Caird, G. B. "The First and Second Books of Samuel," *The Interpreter's Bible*, vol. 2. Nashville: Abingdon Press, 1953.

Carlson, R. A. *David, the Chosen King*. Uppsala: Almqvist and Wiksell, 1964.

Caspari, Wilhelm. *Die Samuelbücher*. Leipzig: A. Deichertsche, 1926.

Cazelles, Henri S. "David's Monarchy and the Gibeonite Claim," *PEQ*, 87 (1955), pp. 165-75.

Clements, R. *Abraham and David: Gen. 15 and its Meaning for Israelite Tradition*. "Studies in Biblical Theology," second series, no. 5. London: SCM Press, 1967.

Cook, S. A. "Notes on Old Testament History," *JQR*, (9 parts), 17-19 (1905-1907), pp. 782ff., 121ff., 347ff., 528ff., 739ff., 168ff., 342ff., 363ff., 383ff.

Cooke, G. "The Israelite King as Son of God," *ZAW*, 73 (1961), pp. 202-25.

Cross, Frank M. "A New Qumran Biblical Fragment Related to the Original Hebrew Underlying the Septuagint," *BASOR*, 132 (1953), pp. 15-26.

_____. "The Oldest Manuscripts from Qumran," *JBL*, 74 (1955), pp. 147ff.

_____. "The Structure of the Deuteronomic History," *Perspectives in Jewish Learning*, edited by J. M. Rosenthal, (Chicago: College of Jewish Studies Press, 1967).

Curtis, John Briggs. "East is East...," *JBL*, 80 (1961), pp. 355ff.

Davies, G. Henton. "Judges 8:22-23," *VT*, 13 (1963), pp. 151-57.

Dion, H. M. "The Patriarchal Traditions and the Literary Form of The Oracle of Salvation," *CBQ*, 29 (1967), pp. 198-206.

Dornseiff, Franz. "Archilochos von Paros und Saul von Gibea," *TLZ*, 80 (1955), p. 499.

Driver, S. R. *A Critical and Exegetical Commentary on Deuteronomy*. *ICC*. Edinburgh: T. and T. Clark, 1895.

_____. *An Introduction to the Literature of the Old Testament*. New York: Meridian, 1956, original edition, 1897.

_____. *Notes on the Hebrew Text and the Topography of the Books of Samuel*, 2nd edition. Oxford: Clarendon Press, 1913.

_____. *A Treatise on the Use of the Tenses in Hebrew*. Oxford: Clarendon Press, 1892.

Eichrodt, Walter. *Theology of the Old Testament*, 2 vols., translated by J. A. Baker. Philadelphia: Westminster, 1961 and 1967.

Eissfeldt, Otto. *Geschichtsschreibung im Alten Testament*. Berlin: Evangelische Verlagsanstalt, 1948.

_____. *The Hebrew Kingdom*. *Cambridge Ancient History*, fasc. 32. Cambridge: University Press, 1965.

Eissfeldt, Otto. *Die Komposition der Samuelisbücher*. Leipzig: J. C. Hinrichs, 1931.

_____. "Noch einmal: Text-, Stil- und Literarkritik in den Samuelisbüchern," *OLZ*, 31 (1928), col. 801ff.

_____. *The Old Testament: An Introduction*, translated by P. Ackroyd. New York: Harper and Row, 1965.

Emerton, J. A. "Review: E. Kutsch, *Salbung als Rechtsakt im Alten Testament und im alten Orient*," *JSS*, 12 (1967), pp. 122f.

Eybers, I. H. "Notes on the Texts of Samuel found in Qumran Cave 4," *Studies on the Book of Samuel*. Stellenbosch, South Africa, 1960.

Finkelstein, E. "An Ignored Haplography in I Sam. 20:23," *JSS*, 4 (1959), pp. 346-57.

Fohrer, Georg. "Die Gattung der Berichte über symbolische Handlungen der Propheten," *ZAW*, 64 (1952), pp. 101-20.

_____. "Der Vertrag zwischen König und Volk in Israel," *ZAW*, 71 (1959), pp. 1-22.

Gadd, C. J. *Ideas of Divine Rule in the Ancient Near East*. London: Oxford University Press, 1948.

Galling, K. "Der Beichtspiegel: eine gattungsgeschichtliche Studie," *ZAW*, 47 (1929), pp. 125-30.

Gehman, H. S. "Exegetical Methods Employed by the Greek Translator of I Samuel," *JAOS*, 70 (1950), pp. 292-96.

Glück, J. J. "Nagid-Shepherd," *VT*, 13 (1963), pp. 144-50.

Good, E. M. *Irony in the Old Testament*. Philadelphia: Westminster, 1965.

Gray, J. "The Hebrew Conception of the Kingship of God," *VT*, 6 (1956), pp. 268-87.

Gressmann, Hugo. "Die älteste Geschichtsschreibung und Prophetie Israels von Samuel bis Amos und Hosea," *Die Schriften des Alten Testaments*, part 2, vol. 1. Göttingen: Vandenhoeck und Ruprecht, 1921.

Habel, N. "The Form and Significance of the Call Narratives," *ZAW*, 77 (1965), pp. 297-323.

Hauer, Christian E. "Does I Samuel 9:1-11:15 Reflect the Extension of Saul's Dominions?" *JBL*, 86 (1967), pp. 406-310.

_____. "The Shape of the Saulide Strategy," *CBQ*, 31 (1969), pp. 153-67.

163

Herrmann, S. "Die Königsnovelle in Ägypten und in Israel," *Wissenschaftliche Zeitschrift der Karl Marx Universität*, Leipzig, 1953/54, pp. 51ff.

Hertzberg, Hans Wilhelm. *I and II Samuel*, translated by J. S. Bowden. Philadelphia: Westminster, 1964.

Hoftijzer, J. "Remarks Concerning the Use of the Particle 't in Classical Hebrew," *Oudtestamentische Studiën*, 14 (1965), pp. 1-99.

Hölscher, Gustav. *Geschichtsschreibung in Israel*. Lund: C. W. K. Gleerup, 1952.

Hylander, Ivar. *Der Literarische Samuel-Saul-Komplex (I Sam. 1-15)*. Uppsala: Almqvist and Wiksell, 1932.

Irwin, W. A. "Samuel and the Rise of the Monarchy," *AJSL*, 58 (1941), pp. 113-34.

Jackson, J. J. "David's Throne: Patterns in the Succession Story," *Canadian Journal of Theology*, 11 (1965), p. 183ff.

James, Fleming. *Personalities of the Old Testament*. New York: Charles Scribner's Sons, 1939.

Jastrow, Morris. "The Name of Samuel and the Stem שאל," *JBL*, 19 (1900), pp. 82ff.

Kapelrud, A. S. "King David and the Sons of Saul," *The Sacral Kingship*. Leiden: E. J. Brill, 1959.

Kaufmann, Yehezkel. *The Religion of Israel*, translated and abridged by M. Greenberg. Chicago: University of Chicago Press, 1960.

Keeley, C. "An Approach to the Books of Samuel," *CBQ*, 10 (1948), pp. 254-70.

Kennedy, A. R. S. *Samuel*. *New Century Bible*. New York: Henry Frowde, 1905.

Knierim, Rolf P. *Die Hauptbegriffe für Sünde im Alten Testament*. Gütersloh: Gütersloher Verlagshaus Gerd Mohn, 1965.

_____. "The Messianic Concept in the First Book of Samuel," *Jesus and the Historian*, edited by F. Thomas Trotter. Philadelphia: Westminster Press, 1968.

Koch, K. *Was Ist Formgeschichte*? Neukirchen: Neukirchener Verlag, 1964.

Kraus, H. J. *Der prophetische Verkündigung des Rechts in Israel*. Zürich: Evangelischer Verlag, 1957.

_____. *Worship in Israel*. Translated by G. Buswell. Richmond: John Knox Press, 1966.

Kutsch, Ernst. *Salbung als Rechtsakt im Alten Testament und im Alten Orient*, BZAW, 87. Berlin: A. Töpelmann, 1963.

_____. "Die Wurzel עצר im Hebräischen," *VT*, 2 (1952), p. 57.

Labuschagne, C. J. *The Incomparability of Yahweh in the Old Testament*. Leiden: E. J. Brill, 1966.

Laurentin, André. "We 'attah-Kai nun. Formule caractéristique des textes juridiques et liturgiques, *Biblica*, 45 (1964), pp. 168-97.

Lindars, B. "Gideon and Kingship," *JTS*, 16 (1965), pp. 315-26.

Lindblom, J. "Lot-casting in the Old Testament," *VT*, 12 (1962), pp. 164-78.

Lods, Adolphe. *Israel from its Beginnings to the Middle of the Eighth Century*, translated by S. H. Hooke. New York: Alfred Knopf, 1948.

Lohfink, N. Review of K. Baltzer, *Das Bundesformular*, in *Scholastik*, 36 (1961), pp. 419-25.

Long, Burke. *The Problem of Etiological Narrative in the Old Testament*, BZAW, 108. Berlin: Töpelmann, 1968.

Macholz, G. *Untersuchungen zur Geschichte der Samuel-Überlieferungen*. Theol. dissertation, Heidelberg, 1966.

Malamat, A. "Doctrines of Causality in Hittite and Biblical Historiography," *VT*, 5 (1955), pp. 1-12.

McCarthy, Dennis J. "II Samuel 7 and the Structure of the Deuteronomic History," *JBL*, 84 (1965), p. 131.

_____. *Treaty and Covenant*. Rome: Pontifical Biblical Institute, 1963.

McKane, William. *I and II Samuel*. London: SCM Press, 1963.

McKenzie, D. A. "The Judge of Israel," *VT*, 17 (1967), pp. 118-21.

_____. *Dictionary of the Bible*. Milwaukee: Bruce Publishing Co., 1965.

_____. "The Dynastic Oracle: II Sam. 7," *TS*, 8 (1947), pp. 187-218.

_____. "The Elders in the Old Testament," *Biblica*, 40 (1959), pp. 522-40.

_____. "The Four Samuels," *BR*, 7 (1962), pp. 3-18.

Mendelsohn, Isaac. "Samuel's Denunciation of Kingship in the Light of Akkadian Documents from Ugarit," *BASOR*, 143 (1956), pp. 17-22.

Merrill, Arthur L. *I Sam. 1-12: A Traditio-historical Study*, Univ. of Chicago Dissertation, 1963.

Mildenberger, F. *Die vordeuteronomistische Saul-David-überlieferung*. Diss. Tübingen, 1962. Cf. *ThLZ*, 87 (1962), col. 778f.

Möhlenbrink, Kurt. "Sauls Ammoniterfeldzug und Samuel's Beitrag zum Königtum des Saul," *ZAW*, 17 (1940-41), pp. 57ff.

Moran, W. L. "A Study of the Deuteronomic History," *Biblica*, 46 (1965), pp. 223-28.

Morgenstern, Julian. "David and Jonathan," *JBL*, 78 (1959), pp. 322-25.

Mowinckel, S. "General Oriental and Specific Israelite Elements in the Israelite Conception of the Sacral Kingdom," *The Sacral Kingship*. Supplement IV to *Numen*. Leiden: E. J. Brill, 1959, pp. 285-93.

_____. "Israelite Historiography," *Annual of the Swedish Theological Institute*, vol. 2. Edited by Hans Komsala. Leiden: E. J. Brill, 1963.

Muilenburg, James. "The Form and Structure of the Covenantal Formulations," *VT*, 9 (1959), pp. 347-65.

_____. "The Linguistic and Rhetorical Usages of the Particle כי in the Old Testament," *HUCA*, 32 (1961), pp. 135ff.

_____. "Mizpah of Benjamin," *StTh*, 8 (1955), pp. 25-42.

_____. Chapters III and IV in *Tell en-Naṣbeh*, edited by C. C. McCown. New Haven: American Schools of Oriental Research, 1947.

Mulder, E. S. "The Prophecy of Nathan in 2 Sam. 7," *Studies on the Books of Samuel*. Stellenbosch, South Africa, 1960.

Myers, J. M. "Saul," *IDB*, edited by G. A. Buttrick. Nashville: Abingdon Press, 1962.

Newman, Murray. "The Prophetic Call of Samuel," *Israel's Prophetic Heritage*, edited by B. W. Anderson and W. Harrelson. New York: Harper and Bros., 1962.

Nicholson, E. W. *Deuteronomy and Tradition*. Philadelphia: Fortress Press, 1967.

Nielsen, E. "The Burial of the Foreign Gods," *StTh*, 8 (1955), pp. 103-22.

166

Nielsen, E. *Shechem: A Traditio-Historical Investigation*. Copenhagen: G.E.C. Gad, 1954.

North, C. R. "The Old Testament Estimate of the Monarchy," *AJSL*, 48 (1931-32), pp. 1-19.

_____. "The Religious Aspects of Hebrew Kingship," *ZAW*, 50 (1932), pp. 3-38.

Noth, Martin. *The History of Israel*, second edition, translated by P. Ackroyd. New York: Harper and Brothers, 1960.

_____. *The Laws in the Pentateuch and Other Studies*, translated by D. R. Ap-Thomas. Edinburgh: Oliver and Boyd, 1966.

_____. *Überlieferungsgeschichtliche Studien*, second edition. Tübingen: Max Niemeyer, 1957.

Oberholzer, J. R. "The 'ibrim in I Samuel," *Studies on the Books of Samuel*. Stellenbosch, South Africa, 1960.

Oberhuber, K. "Zur Syntax des Richterbuches. Der einfache Nominalsatz und die sog. nominale Apposition," *VT*, 3 (1953), p. 41.

Pederson, Johannes. *Israel: Its Life and Culture*, 2 vols. London: Oxford Univ. Press, 1926.

Pfeiffer, R. H. *Introduction to the Old Testament*, revised edition. New York: Harper and Brothers, 1941.

Press, Richard. "Der Prophet Samuel. Eine traditionsgeschichtliche Untersuchung," *ZAW*, 56 (1938), pp. 177ff.

_____. "Sauls Königswahl," *TB*, 12 (1933), pp. 243-48.

von Rad, Gerhard. *Deuteronomy*, translated by Dorothea Barton. Philadelphia: Westminster Press, 1966.

_____. "The Early History of the Form-Category of I Cor. 13:4-7," *The Problem of the Hexateuch and Other Essays*, translated by E. W. Trueman Dicken. New York: McGraw-Hill, 1966.

_____. *Der Heilige Krieg im alten Israel*. Zürich: Zwingli, 1951.

_____. *Old Testament Theology*, 2 vols., translated by D. M. G. Stalker. New York: Harper and Brothers, 1962 and 1965.

_____. "The Royal Ritual of Judah," *The Problem of the Hexateuch and Other Essays*, translated by E. W. Trueman Dicken. New York: McGraw-Hill, 1966.

_____. *Studies in Deuteronomy*. "Studies in Biblical Theology," no. 9. London: SCM Press, 1953.

Rahtjen, B. D. "Philistine and Hebrew Amphictyonies," *JNES*, 24 (1962), pp. 100-04.

Rendtorff, R. "Reflections on the Early History of Prophecy in Israel," *History and Hermeneutics*, edited by Robert Funk. Translated by P. Achtemeir. New York: Harper and Row, 1967, pp. 14ff.

_____. *Studien zur Geschichte des Opfers im alten Israel*. Neukirchen: Neukirchener Verlag, 1967.

Richter, Wolfgang. *Die Bearbeitungen des 'Retterbuches' in der Deuteronomischen Epoche. Bonner Biblische Beiträge*, 21. Bonn: Peter Hanstein, 1965.

_____. "Die *nagid*-Formel," *BZ*, 9 (1965), pp. 71-84.

_____. *Traditionsgeschichtliche Untersuchungen zum Richterbuch. Bonner Biblische Beiträge*, 18. Bonn: Peter Hanstein, 1963.

Riemann, Paul. "The Sources for the Establishment of the Kingship in I Samuel," unpublished paper. Graduate Seminar, Harvard University, 1959.

Ritterspach, Austin David. *The Samuel Traditions: An Analysis of the Anti-Monarchical Source in I Samuel 1-15*. Unpublished dissertation, The Graduate Theological Union, 1967.

Robertson, Edward. *The Old Testament Problem*. Manchester: University Press, 1950.

_____. "Samuel and Saul," *BJRL*, 28 (1944), pp. 175-206.

Rosenthal, E. I. J. "Some Aspects of the Hebrew Monarchy," *JJS*, 9 (1958), pp. 1-18.

Saydon, P. P. "Assonance in Hebrew as a Means of Expressing Emphasis," *Biblica*, 36 (1955), pp. 36-50, 287-304.

Schildenberger, J. "Zur Einleitung in die Samuelbücher," *Miscellanea Biblica et Orientalia*, edited by R. P. Athanasio Miller. *Studia Anselmia* 27-38.

Schmidt, Werner H. "Die Deuteronomistische Redaktion des Amosbuches," *ZAW*, 77 (1965), pp. 168-93.

_____. *Königtum Gottes in Ugarit und Israel. BZAW*, 80. Berlin: A. Töpelmann, 1961.

Schunck, Klaus-Dietrich. *Benjamin. BZAW*, 86. Berlin: A. Töpelmann, 1963.

Seebass, H. "I Sam. 15 als Schlüssel für das Verständnis der sogenannten königsfreundlichen Reihe I Sam. 9:1-10:16, 11:1-15, und 13:2-14:52," *ZAW*, 78 (1966), pp. 149ff.

Seebass, H. "Traditionsgeschichte von I Sam. 8, 10:17ff., und
    12," *ZAW*, 77 (1965), pp. 286ff.

_____. "Die Vorgeschichte der Königserhebung Sauls," *ZAW*,
    79 (1967), pp. 155ff.

_____. "Zum Text von I Sam. 14:23b-25a und 2:29, 31-33,"
    VT, 16 (1966), pp. 74-82.

Seeligmann, I. L. "Hebräische Erzählung und biblische Ge-
    schichtsschreibung," *TZ*, 18 (1962), pp. 305-25.

van Selms, A. "The Armed Forces of Israel under Saul and
    David," *Studies on the Books of Samuel*. Stellenbosch,
    South Africa, 1960.

Smith, H. P. *A Critical and Exegetical Commentary on the Books
    of Samuel. International Critical Commentary*. New York:
    Charles Scribner's Sons, 1902.

Snaith, Norman. "The Historical Books," *The Old Testament and
    Modern Study*, edited by H. H. Rowley. Oxford: Oxford
    University Press, 1956.

Soggin, J. A. "Charisma und Institution im Konigtum Sauls,"
    ZAW, 75 (1963), pp. 54-65.

Speiser, E. A. "An Analogue to 2 Sam. 1:21, AQHT 1:44-45,"
    JBL, 69 (1950), pp. 377-78.

Spiro, A. "The Vilification of King Saul in Biblical Litera-
    ture," *JBL*, 71 (1952), p. ix.

Stoebe, Hans Joachim. "Anmerkungen zu I Sam. 8:16 und 16:20,"
    VT, 4 (1954), pp. 177ff.

_____. "David und Mikal. Überlegungen zur Jugendgeschichte
    Davids," *Von Ugarit nach Qumran*, edited by J. Hempel and
    Leonhard Rost. *BZAW*, 77. Berlin: A. Töpelmann, 1958,
    pp. 224ff.

_____. "Die Goliathperikope I Sam. 17:1-18:5 und die Text-
    form der Septuaginta," *VT*, 6 (1956), pp. 397-413.

_____. "Noch einmal die Eselinnen des Kis," *VT*, 7 (1957),
    pp. 362-70.

Szikszai, S. "Samuel," and "Samuel, I and II," *IDB*, edited by
    G. A. Buttrick. Nashville: Abingdon Press, 1962.

Thornton, T. C. G. "Charismatic Kingship in Israel and Ju-
    dah," *JTS*, 14 (1963), pp. 1-11.

Tiktin, H. *Kritische Untersuchungen zu den Büchern Samuelis*.
    Göttingen: Vandenhoeck und Ruprecht, 1922.

Tsevat, M. "The Biblical Narrative of the Foundation of Kingship in Israel, I Sam. 8-12," (Hebr.), *Tarbiz*, 36 (1966-67), pp. 99-109.

de Vaux, Roland. *Ancient Israel: Its Life and Institutions*, translated by John McHugh. London: Darton, Longman and Todd, 1961.

_____. "Les Combats Singuliers dans l'Ancien Testament," *Biblica*, 40 (1959), pp. 495-508.

_____. *Les Livres de Samuel*. Paris, 1953.

_____. "Le roi d'Israel, vassal de Yahvé," *Mélanges Eugène Tisserant*, vol. I. Rome, 1964, pp. 119-33.

Wallis, G. "Eine Parallele zu Richter 19:29ff. und I Sam. 11:5ff. aus dem Briefarchiv von Mari," *ZAW*, 64 (1952), pp. 57-61.

Weiser, Artur. "I Sam. 15," *ZAW*, 54 (1936), pp. 1ff.

_____. *The Old Testament: Its Formation and Development*. New York: Association Press, 1961.

_____. *Samuel: Seine geschichtliche Aufgabe und religiöse Bedeutung*. Göttingen: Vandenhoeck und Ruprecht, 1962.

_____. "Samuel und die Vorgeschichte des israelitischen Königtums," *ZThK*, 57 (1960), pp. 141-61.

_____. "Samuel's 'Philister-Sieg': Die Überlieferungen in I Samuel 7," *ZThK*, 56 (1959), pp. 253ff.

Welch, Adam C. *Kings and Prophets of Israel*. London: Lutterworth Press, 1952.

Wellhausen, Julius. *Die Composition des Hexateuchs und der historischen Bücher des Alten Testaments*. Berlin, 1899.

_____. *Prolegomena to the History of Ancient Israel*. Translated by Menzies and Black. New York: Meridian, 1957, original German edition, 1878.

_____. *Der Text der Bücher Samuelis*. Göttingen: Vandenhoeck und Ruprecht, 1872.

Westermann, Claus. *Basic Forms of Prophetic Speech*, translated by Hugh C. White. Philadelphia: Westminster Press, 1967.

Whitley, C. F. "The Sources of the Gideon Stories," *VT*, 7 (1957), pp. 157-64.

Wildberger, H. "Samuel und die Entstehung des israelitischen Königtums," *TZ*, 13 (1957), pp. 442ff.

Williams, James G. "The Prophetic Father: A Brief Explanation of the Term 'Sons of the Prophets'," *JBL*, 85 (1966), pp. 344ff.

Wolff, Hans Walter. "Das Kerygma des deuteronomistischen Geschichtswerks," *ZAW*, 73 (1961), pp. 171ff.

_____. *Das Zitat im Prophetenspruch*. Munich: C. Kaiser, 1937.

Wright, G. Ernest. "Fresh Evidence for the Philistine Story," *BA*, 29 (1966), pp. 70-86.

Würthwein, E. "Der Ursprung der prophetischen Gerichtsrede," *ZThK*, 41 (1952), pp. 1-16.

van Zyl, A. H. "Israel and the Indigenous Population of Canaan according to the Books of Samuel," *Studies on the Books of Samuel*. Stellenbosch, South Africa, 1960.

°295-3
5-13
CC

*296-3
5-13
CC